TRUE EVANGELISM

ALSO BY LEWIS SPERRY CHAFER

Grace: An Exposition of God's Marvelous Gift
Salvation: God's Marvelous Work of Grace
Satan: His Motives and Methods
Systematic Theology

TRUE EVANGELISM

*Winning Souls
Through Prayer*

Lewis Sperry Chafer

True Evangelism: Winning Souls Through Prayer
by Lewis Sperry Chafer

Published in 1993 by Kregel Publications, a division of Kregel, Inc., 2450 Oak Industrial Dr. NE, Grand Rapids, MI 49505.

Library of Congress Cataloging-in-Publication Data
Chafer, Lewis Sperry, 1871-1952.
   True Evangelism: Winning Souls Through Prayer / Lewis Sperry Chafer.
        p.   cm.
   Originally published: Rev. ed. Philadelphia: Sunday School Times Co., 1919.
   Includes index.
   1. Evangelistic work. 2. Prayer—Christianity. I. Title.
BV3790.C47   1993   269'.2—dc20   92-44075

ISBN 978-0-8254-4372-5

Printed in the United States of America

Contents

Introduction to the First Edition

If there is sufficient warrant for this book, in addition to the many already written on Evangelism, it lies in the effort which is here made to place an emphasis upon the fact that evangelism is the service of the whole company of believers, and that when they intelligently cooperate with the Spirit in this work, there is less demand for the modern evangelist or his methods.

What is here written is the result of evangelistic experience and study covering a period of almost a score of years. During this time the trend of the writer's conviction has been away from emotional and superficial methods, which are too often thought to be the only possible expression of earnestness and enthusiasm in soul-winning, and toward an entire dependence upon the Spirit to do every phase of the work that has been assigned to Him in the purpose of God.

It is not a pleasant task to offer criticism of any faithful effort in evangelism; for a sincere attempt to reach the lost, though misguided, is preferable to the spiritual death and formalism which knows no burden or sacrifice for the unsaved. What may seem as criticism has been introduced only where it is needed to emphasize true evangelism by way of contrast. It is intended that this work shall be constructive rather than critical. If some of the difficulties in soul-winning, with the divine provisions to overcome them, are herein revealed, and any new light shall fall on the exact responsibility

7

of the individual Christian in co-operation with Christ, and that new light be acted upon, the going forth of this testimony in the name of Christ and for His glory will not have been in vain.

LEWIS SPERRY CHAFER

1911

Foreword to the First Edition

Your welcome letter from Northfield found me in much physical pain and weakness. The more welcome may I say on this account, for should my brotherly words in reference to your timely volume prove to be my latest, I would be grateful for their occasion. The proof pages read at the early stages of convalescence have been greatly valued and enjoyed. The standard is, as it should be, high, true, clear, and unmistakably loyal to the revelation of God.

Your volume, in my judgment, is of great value. I praise God for your writing. The ministry of the Holy Spirit is clearly revealed in the luminous pages of *True Evangelism*. I heartily endorse and rejoice in the prominence to the unchanging character of human salvation effected at the instance and by the power of the living God in Christ Jesus the Lord.

The distinct revelation given from the Word of God is admirable. You have not failed to "hold fast the form of sound words," which the Spirit of God maintains in the New Testament. These can never be changed, modified, or made to teach the crude fallacies of "modern criticism," or "New Theology."

Needless to say, you have revealed the cause of much failure in past evangelistic effort. Despite these failures, we will never forget that it is written of the exalted Lord that He gave some apostles, some prophets, some evangelists, some pastors and teachers for the perfecting of the saints to the work of the ministry, to the edifying of the Body of Christ (Eph. 4:11, 12). That the god of this age will counterfeit the real gifts is certain, the modern sacrificing priest and the mere professional evangelist yielding conclusive proof.

Many years since, in conversation with our glorified friend, C. H. Spurgeon, the question came up, of what our part was, or could be, in connection with the salvation of men, seeing that the fact and glory of their salvation belonged entirely to Christ.

I remember expressing the following, "that real and personal fellowship in the compassionate love and sufferings of Christ in regard to the salvation of others might yield partnership in that glory which by right alone belongs to our Lord."

With the structure and the furtherance of your theme, as indicated by the titles of the successive chapters, I am in hearty agreement. Your searching words in relation to certain phases of modern evangelism, both as to men and methods, should cause deep searching of heart; nor must we fail to point out what poor "soul-winners" at best we all are. Our cry must be: "O Lord, be with us, and help us, for without Thee we can do nothing."

HENRY VARLEY

Author's note:

The above foreword proved to be the last written words of Mr. Varley. He passed on two days later to be with Christ.

Foreword to the Revised Edition

If the reputation of the author be not yet continentally established, a foreword to his book may be useful. *True Evangelism,* when first published, bore on its pages a reassuring and discriminating appreciation from one of the most trusted and successful evangelists of our time. Rev. Lewis Sperry Chafer since then has achieved outstanding distinction both as Bible teacher and author. What further good purpose can another foreword to this new and revised edition serve? To "born again" ones who read the book studiously and reverently (and no other can understand it, whatever their education, theological or otherwise, 1 Cor. 2:14) little or none; but to those who may be in a similar mental condition toward books on evangelism as that in which the undersigned found himself when he first glanced through this book in a book store, it may be like the voice the great Angustine heard, "Take and read"—and if it induces them to read, then they will know the profit.

At that time I had not the joy and enrichment of a personal acquaintance with the author, whose friendship, love and brotherly counsel have been one of God's choicest gifts to me in the past four years. The title attracted me, for my estimation of the surpassing importance of the subject had led me to purchase almost every book on this theme that had come to my notice. However, so often I had been disappointed with the unsatisfactory and unscriptural character of many of these, that I had passed the buying-at-sight stage. Arrested by the thoughtful and evangelical tone of the foreword, I began to sample its pages and found that it promised to be a book with a distinctive, timely, and Scriptural message on this vital theme. A careful reading followed, which more than justified the forecast I had made. So many other books on this subject were disappointing, not because they were lacking in style, vivacity or popular phraseology, but because vitally lacking in spiritual interpretation, especially concerning the two great master ideas of God's Holy Word, *Sin* and *Redemption*. Jerome, in the fourth century, declared that "light views of sin induced false views of God," and the late master-preacher, MacLaren of Manchester, stated that "ninety percent of all doctrinal errors have grown up around defective views of sin." Any theory that minimizes sin minimizes the redemptive work of our Lord Jesus Christ and the regenerative work of the Holy Spirit. Such theory also must make a large appeal to men (almost betimes as frantic as that of the Prophets of Baal on Carmel's summit), and clever little devices have been invented to induce men to "take Christ," or "step over the line," and which offer to settle the great eternal question by an oral acceptance of a simple synthesis, or of a little formula on a small printed card.

One turns from these naturalistic, legalistic, colorless conceptions of sin and salvation to this precious book with its grave, thorough, Biblical treatment of Man's sin and God's salvation, and finds his heart full of praise to God for empowering His humble and honored servant to send forth a message so virile, timely, and throbbing with power.

May the Triune God, Whose Word and grace it magnifies, speed this unpretentious book on its beneficent mission, that by His grace and power it may accomplish what He pleases, and hasten the coming and Kingdom of our Lord and Savior, Jesus Christ.

A. B. WINCHESTER

Toronto, May 20, 1919

Chapter 1

False Forces in Evangelism

The Lord Jesus described His mission by the words: "For the Son of Man is come to seek and to save that which was lost" (Luke 19:10), and this concise statement included both His finished work upon the cross (John 19:30), and His unfinished work in the world (Acts 1:1). While the work of saving the lost must ever be a divine undertaking accomplished only through His finished work on the cross, there are aspects of the work of seeking them which were committed to His followers, and which are a part of His unfinished work in the world.

The work of seeking the lost, like the work of saving them, is in reality a divine undertaking. It is distinctly stated that the Son of Man is come to seek. Thus He is again pictured in the Parable of the Lost Sheep: "When he has found it, he lays it upon his shoulders, rejoicing." It is the "goodness of God that leads to repentance," and the whole undertaking of finding lost men is but "the power of God unto salvation"; for no human effort or service can be effectual apart from the power of God. Seeking the lost is more than a mere attempt to locate unsaved men, for they are present on every hand. The term "seeking the lost," therefore, suggests a divine preparation of the unsaved that will bring them into adjustment with the necessary conditions of salvation.

It will be found, in the course of these studies, that there are successive aspects of the divine seeking of the lost to be traced in the Scriptures, and every phase of this work is undertaken and wholly accomplished by God the Holy Spirit. To recognize these divine movements and to be willing humbly to cooperate with them is the true basis of all soul-saving work.

While it has pleased God to appoint to His saints (not as a corporate body, but as individuals) a portion in the work of seeking, the human part in that work is not worthy to be compared with the divine. Yet man, who by nature comprehends and measures only visible things, is ever prone to disregard the invisible working of the Spirit, and to place an undue emphasis upon the comparatively small human share in those undertakings.

It is under these distorted estimates of the factors in the work of salvation that those things which may be called "false forces" in evangelism are substituted for the true. What are here termed "false forces" are, in some measure, God-appointed means in true evangelism. They become false forces only when they receive too much emphasis, or are strained to perform a function beyond that assigned to them in the purpose of God. Thus it may be seen that failure in evangelism is not always due to an entire neglect of some part, or parts, of the divine appointments for the work; but may be due to an unbalanced estimate of the relative values of these forces.

This discussion of false forces in evangelism will be limited to three general aspects—viz., Men, Methods, and Messages.

Men

By this term reference is made to a class of men in the ministry called "evangelists," and on whom the church has come to depend so largely for her activity in evangelism.

The word "evangelist" is used but three times in the Scriptures, and but one of these passages is to any extent descriptive. It is as follows: "Wherefore he saith, when he ascended on high, he led captivity captive, and gave gifts unto men.

"And he gave some to be apostles; and some, prophets; and some, evangelists; and some, pastors and teachers; for the perfecting of the saints, unto the work of ministering, unto the building up of the body of Christ: till we all attain unto the unity of the faith, and of the knowledge of the Son of God, unto a full grown man, unto the measure of the stature of the fullness of Christ" (Eph. 4:8, 11-13, A.V.).

Here the evangelist is seen, with the apostle, prophet, pastor and teacher, to be a gift of the ascended Christ to His church in the world. This ministry gift of the apostle, prophet, evangelist, and pastor and teacher should be distinguished from the enduement for service bestowed upon the individual believer (1 Cor. 12:4-31; Rom. 12:3-8). In the one case the servant of God who has been endued for ministry is Christ's gift to the whole church; while in the other case a special enablement for service is given to the individual believer by the sovereign Spirit "as he will."

In this same connection still another distinction should be made, in that the believer, in addition to the exercise of gifts, is appointed to the ministry of the priestly office; and since evangelism will be found to depend so largely upon the exercise of the believer's gifts and his ministry in the priestly office, a violation has been done to the plan of God, as revealed in His Word, insomuch as the work of evangelism has been taken from the whole company of believers and entrusted to a few.

The evangelist of the Scriptures is, without question, the messenger to the unevangelized, preparing the way for the pastor and teacher in his more constant ministry in the church. The evangelist, therefore, finds his fullest divine mission as a pioneer missionary to the hitherto unevangelized.

The modern "revival"—the work of the "revivalist" who comes under the title of an evangelist, but works as a religious promoter in the organized church—is unexpected in the Scriptures, except as the word "revival" is used to denote a forward movement in the spiritual life of the church, without including the idea of attempting to regain some spiritual position once held, but now lost. The use of the word usually means, however, a getting up after having fallen down, or a waking after sleeping, or a coming to strength after a period of weakness; while, on the other hand, the Scriptures pre-suppose a continual erect, wakeful and aggressive position for service on the part of every Christian (Eph. 6:10-17). A "revival" is abnormal rather than normal. It may have a function when needed, but in no way should become a habit, much less a sanctioned method of work. Having regained vitality, believers are not warranted in returning habitually to an anemic state.

The readjustment of a powerless church into a normal position of fruit-bearing fellowship with God is, without question, an undertaking that is warranted in the Scriptures. Such a transformation, however, can be accomplished only through a ministry of teaching and pastoral care. Thus it falls naturally within the sphere of service committed to the pastor and teacher whose ministry is not necessarily located in one place, since he is a gift to the whole body of believers. Such a ministry may be undertaken by a pastor and teacher who is a specialist in such work, and who may visit the field to assist temporarily the resident pastor in his work. If this adjustment of the church is accomplished, the pastor or special assistant may then "do the work of an evangelist." There is an important distinction, however, between being an evangelist by calling, and doing the work of an evangelist as occasion may arise in the pastoral office.

The efficiency of the whole company of believers must depend upon their proper adjustment to God in the cleansing and fitting of their individual lives. Just here there is a grave danger lest the church shall ignore her God-appointed work, and the necessary individual preparation for it, and attempt to substitute the wholesale machinery and appeal of the modern "revival" in its place.

The fact that a "revival" is planned for is a confession on the part of a church of a condition which would render the normal movements of the Spirit in salvation impossible. The special help of a Scriptural evangelist might be imperative in gathering the abundant fruit produced by the faithful evangelizing efforts of a church. It will be admitted, however, that such conditions do not often exist. On the contrary, the sincere and intelligent evangelist, almost without exception, must first do the work of a pastor and teacher by seeking to revive the church itself.

The unfruitful condition of the church has created a great temptation for the evangelist to be superficial in his aim and undertakings. His reputation, and often his remuneration, are dependent upon apparent results. If the evangelist understands the divine program in soul-winning, and proposes to be thorough with unspiritual churches, he must do a teaching work that he may build the necessary Scriptural foundation for abiding fruit. In undertaking a thorough foundation work in the churches, the evangelist would thus be forsaking his own calling, and would be assuming the work of the pastor and teacher; and might be a disappointment to those who had called him and upon whom he depends, humanly speaking, for his support. His temptation is to secure the apparent results that are expected. The work of the evangelist is a vital ministry in this age, but it, like all ministry, should be kept within the sphere divinely appointed for it.

The discussion of the fundamental error of the church, in unduly magnifying the work of the evangelist and neglecting her own God-appointed ministry in salvation, will be the theme of succeeding chapters.

Methods

Likewise, an undue emphasis upon methods in modern evangelism is almost universal. The erroneous impression exists that evangelistic efforts should be confined to stated times and seasons, and that impression has led to a far more serious one, namely, that God is only occasionally "on the giving hand"; whereas the Scriptural forces in true evangelism depend upon the unchanging promises of God, the constant abiding presence of the Holy Spirit in the Church, and His continual working through the members of the body of Christ.

Frequent gatherings may be of unmeasured value in the life of any company of believers; but such meetings should not become the only time of soul-winning expectation. The conditions are most unreasonable when the unbelievers of any locality have come to realize that to avoid the spasmodic solicitude of the church for a period of a few days is to be free from such appeals for the rest of the year, or for, perhaps, a term of years. This unreality is one of the fruits of an evangelism that depends upon times and seasons.

Again, the false or undue emphasis on methods is disclosed by the imperative demand for some public action in connection with conversion, such as standing or going forward in a meeting. Great confusion has been wrought by the intrusion of such public acts into the condition for salvation—thereby making salvation seem to be by faith in Christ, plus a supposedly meritorious public act.

These required public acts are usually justified from one or two passages of Scripture, which are here quoted: "Whosoever therefore shall confess me before men, him will I confess also before my Father which is in heaven" (Matt. 10:32), and, "That if thou shalt confess with thy mouth the Lord Jesus, and shalt believe in thine heart that God has raised him from the dead, thou shalt be saved. For with the heart man believeth unto righteousness; and with the mouth confession is made unto salvation" (Rom. 10:9, 10).

A careful study of the whole context of the former passage will reveal that the passage occurs in a body of Scripture which is primarily applicable to the yet future Kingdom age, and it, like all that truth, bears only a moral or secondary application to the age of the church. From this particular passage, therefore, confession cannot be made a present condition of salvation.

The second passage quoted above (Rom. 10:9, 10) is perhaps more important, since it falls within the teachings and conditions which belong primarily to the soul under grace.

The force of the positive statement in verse 9, "If thou shalt confess with thy mouth the Lord Jesus, and shalt believe in thine heart that God has raised him from the dead, thou shalt be saved," is explained in verse 10: "For with the heart man believeth unto righteousness, and with the mouth confession is made unto salvation." In the latter verse the true meaning and use of the word "confess" is suggested. Of this word in this same passage the late Dr. Arthur T. Pierson wrote: "That word means to speak out of a like nature to one another. I believe and receive the love of God. In receiving His love I receive His life, in receiving His life I receive His nature, and His nature in me naturally expresses itself according to His will. That is confession. Dr. MeLareu has said: 'Men do not light a candle and put it under a bushel, because the candle would either go out or burn the bushel.' You must have vent for life, light and love, or how can they abide? And a confession of Christ Jesus as Lord is the answer of the new life of God received. In receiving love, you are born of God, and, being born of God, you cry, 'Abba, Father,' which is but the Aramaic word for 'Papa'— syllables which can be pronounced before there are any teeth, because they are made with the gums and lips—the first word of a new-born soul, born of God, knowing God, and out of a like nature with God speaking in the language of a child."

Confession, then, does not provide a reason for salvation, but rather proves its reality. It is clearly the believer's privilege, and is of no value until Christ has been received and the new life begun.

So with the heart, or inner consciousness, man believes unto righteousness, which is the one condition of acceptance before God; and with the mouth confession is made unto salvation, which is but the normal answer of the new-born soul to God.

That these passages do not demand a public act as a condition of salvation is obvious for at least two other reasons. First, such an interpretation would disagree with all other passages of Scripture on salvation, since it would cause grace to be no more grace, inasmuch as there was saving merit in a human deed; and it is difficult to demand confession in connection with conversion without making it seem to be meritorious, and, to that extent, a frustrating of the whole doctrine of grace. And second, a public confession cannot be a necessity in salvation, since an innumerable company have found fullest peace with God through Christ Jesus who were deprived of the supposed value of any such action.

In coming to a positive decision, the human mind is undoubtedly aided by some physical action which serves to strengthen the impression. This psychological fact usually underlies the demands that are made for public acts in connection with the acceptance of Christ. The only issue which is raised here concerning the combining of public acts with the acceptance of Christ, is that such acts, if urged at all, should be so presented that they could not be thought of by any individual as forming a part of the one condition of salvation. To believe on the Lord Jesus Christ is the very opposite of doing anything: it is resting in the work and saving grace of Another.

Because of Satanic blindness to the Gospel of Grace (2 Cor. 4:3, 4), unregenerate man cannot comprehend the true basis of salvation, and is therefore ever prone to do the best he knows. This is to attempt to work out his own standing before God by his own efforts. It is this natural tendency to do something of merit that prompts many to respond to any appeal for a public action. It was an expression of sincerity that inquired of Jesus: "What shall we do, that we might work the works of God?" And His answer then is His answer now: "This is the work of God, that ye believe on him whom he hath sent" (John 6:28,29).

It may be conceded that genuine results are sometimes obtained even where misleading methods are employed; but there may be great harm done as well. Far too little has been said on this point. Some of these evils should be mentioned. Let it be remembered, however, that this is a discussion of the possible evils that may follow the wrong use of methods in which a public action is demanded as a necessary condition of salvation.

I. A False Issue

The leader who has accustomed himself to years of public service can hardly realize the almost impossible task that is placed before the majority of people when they are asked to do some conspicuous act. People usually find such acts very difficult; and while they might be willing to receive Christ as a personal Savior, they often shrink from taking a public step because of their natural timidity. Thus the real issue is many times subordinated to another; and that new issue is not only unreal, but is entirely foreign to the all-important question. In this connection it is often urged that the unsaved should be sufficiently in earnest to comply readily with any method or custom that may be employed. But is it not evident, in addition to the fact that such demands may be a denial of the doctrine of grace, that they are both unwarranted and unreasonable, since God has provided no enabling power whereby unregenerate people may do commendable acts for Him? A public confession is a far different task to the same timid person after he has received the new divine life; for he can then say by faith, and in all humility: "I can do all things through Christ which strengtheneth me" (Phil. 4:13).

The one necessary step—the acceptance of Christ as Savior—can be performed only in the secret of the heart itself, by a personal choice and action of the will. This is a dealing with Christ alone, and as the time of this decision is the most critical moment in a human life, reason demands that it should be guarded from every distracting and confusing condition.

II. A False Assurance

A leader with a commanding personality may secure the public action of many when the issue is made one of religious merit through some public act. Under such an impression, a serious person may stand in a meeting who has no conception of what is involved in standing by faith on the Rock Christ Jesus; or he may be persuaded to abandon his natural timidity when he knows nothing of abandoning his Satanic tendency to self-help, and resting by faith on that which Christ has done for him. If questioned carefully, the basis of assurance with all such converts will be found to be no more than a consciousness that they have acted out the program prescribed for them.

III. "Backsliding"

Careful students of evangelism have noticed that where the necessity of public action as a part of conversion has been most emphasized there has been a corresponding increase in the God-dishonoring record of so-called "backsliding"; and this is natural. The covenant of God is to keep eternally all who are truly saved, and there are no other provisions, than the one way of salvation by Christ's willing substitution, whereby God can be just and still be the justifier of a sin-cursed soul. To attempt to "come unto God" on the grounds of a public performance, even with great earnestness, is but to fail, and the misguided soul who makes that attempt, when his hope has proven false, is often the hardest to reach thereafter.

IV. Discredit to the Covenant of God

As has just been stated, the essential and Scriptural doctrine of the eternal keeping by God of every regenerate soul has been brought into discredit and almost lost. This has come to pass through an attempt to reconcile His covenants with "actual experience" in evangelism today. It has been necessary to question this otherwise clear doctrine of the Scriptures to allow for the appalling percentage of failures in the ranks of supposed converts. But when it is remembered that the modification of that positive doctrine, and the forced interpretation of the Word of God to that end, has been attempted largely by those who have insisted on a spectacular conversion, their challenge of that glorious truth may be set aside without discussion.

Although an innumerable multitude may have been misguided by responding to false issues and have returned, sooner or later, to their own place outside Christian fellowship, the covenant of God is not involved. "Wherefore he is able also to save them to the uttermost [eternally] that come unto God by him"—Christ (Heb. 7:25); He "is able to keep you from falling, and to present you faultless before the presence of his glory with exceeding joy" (Jude 24). And the soul that believes in Christ "shall not come into condemnation; but is passed from death unto life" (John 5:24). Nor can any "pluck them out of my Father's hand" (John 10:29), or separate them "from the love of God, which is in Christ Jesus our Lord" (Rom. 8:39).

It is quite possible for a newly saved person so to misunderstand the forces and habits of the old life and the possible power and victory of the new life as to be overtaken in sin and appear, for a time, to be "in a far country"; yet, if he has ever been in the Father's house as a son, he, like the prodigal, is still a son, and therefore will be constantly constrained by the Spirit to arise and go to his Father.

Incalculable harm has been done to all Christendom by this widespread denial of the grace and faithfulness of God. Because of this denial, saints have been occupied with futile attempts at self-keeping to the neglect of true service for God, and intelligent sinners have feared to take the Christian's position when reason warned them that such a position would be impossible for them to maintain.

V. Dishonor to the Spirit of God

The aim of all public demands in modern evangelism is to terminate indifference and hesitation by a positive decision. But this is sometimes undertaken without due regard for the whole process of preparation by the Spirit for the intelligent exercise of saving faith. Thus the all-important work of the spirit for the unsaved has often been neglected and the Spirit dishonored in the vain attempt to hasten decisions and to secure visible results.

A true decision must depend upon the action of the will of the individual as he is moved by his own clear vision of his place in the saving work of Christ, and that vision must be created by the Spirit. When this is accomplished, there will be little occasion to argue and plead, and methods which are calculated to force a decision will be found to be superfluous; and any method which is superfluous is usually resented by intelligent people. Such methods create a sense of unreality where there should be a growing reality.

Many serious men have concluded that to send out workers to plead with individuals in a miscellaneous congregation is not only embarrassing to the people thus approached, but is, in the majority of cases, a service which hardens and repels. Forced decisions sometimes follow such appeals. These, they observe, are usually premature and unintelligent decisions; for in such methods there can be no certainty concerning the conviction by the Spirit and no very definite dependence upon His leading. On the other hand, the many who have resisted the personal appeal have been hardened or driven away.

Public methods which embarrass any person or class of persons may be not only useless but intrusive. There is little gained by inviting all Christians in a public gathering to stand, thus forcing all others into a conspicuous position, causing them annoyance and creating an occasion for prejudice. It is not strange that intelligent unsaved people sometimes avoid meetings where these methods are employed. By adopting such a program the evangelist or pastor may be hindering the very work of God which he is attempting to do.

If the spectacular element in public soul-winning is eliminated there will be less opportunity to count supposed results, and the test of conversion will be removed from the sphere of profession and made to rest on the reality of a changed life afterwards.

The sincere evangelist who fearlessly judges, before God, every method he employs—judging them as to their exact value or possible harm in their influence on immortal souls—will find that many methods in evangelism are more a habit than a necessity, or that they have been employed in all effort to produce visible results, rather than to create a means by which sin-burdened souls may find rest and peace through a personal and intelligent faith in Christ as Savior.

Lest it seem that this criticism of modern methods in evangelism has left no possible means of bringing a whole congregation to a point of decision, the following suggestions are offered, which have proven useful.

The real value of public methods may be secured and many evils avoided if, after explaining the way of life and during a season of silent prayer, the unsaved are asked to accept Christ by a conscious act of the will, directed in definite silent prayer to God. Such a decision may then be greatly strengthened by an immediate public confession of Christ. The vital difference in question is, however, that such are then confessing that they have believed on Christ, rather than making a confession in order that they may be saved. After such an appeal, an opportunity should be made for personal conversation with any who believe they have accepted Christ by faith, or any others who may have honest difficulties. In this conversation the individual's exact understanding of the step may be ascertained and his faith strengthened. Such conversations may be secured early in an after-meeting, or by offering some attractive literature suited to beginners in the Christian life. When it is clear that an intelligent decision has been made, constant confession of Christ as a personal Savior, should be urged along with the other duties and privileges of the new life.

Messages

In considering *messages* as the last of the three "false forces" in evangelism already mentioned, it may well be restated that the ministry of the New Testament evangelist was intended to be wider in its scope than the accepted mission of the evangelist of today. As his name implies, he is the "bearer of glad tidings," and so is in marked contrast to the prophet who proclaims the great principles of morality and righteousness. He has also a far different mission than the pastor and teacher who shepherds the flock and feeds them on the Word of God.

The New Testament evangelist is given a particular message to proclaim. That message is the "good news" of the Gospel of Grace; it is therefore a distinct body of truth for this age. His evangel is one of "glad tidings," because it offers freedom from the bondage of the law, with attempts at self-fitting for the presence of God, and because it proclaims a perfect salvation by the power of God through faith in Jesus Christ and His redemption by the cross— salvation through which God by His power produces a "new creature," able, because of the new life imparted, to bring forth fruit to His glory.

Any deviation from this prescribed message of redemptive truth is an unwarranted undertaking on the part of the evangelist, and is fraught with grave dangers. On the one hand, he may be tempted to adopt the message of the prophet; or he may undertake the work of the pastor and teacher and deal with matters of Christian living, and thus encumber the glorious but limited message of the evangelist. For the issue before the unsaved is not one of after-conduct. The life to be led after conversion can be determined only by the individual himself in the light and power of the new relation to Christ, Whom he has received and the manner of that new life is a personal matter between the Christian and his Lord (Rom. 14:4). Yet, when dealing with the unsaved, the questions which belong to Christian living, such as forms of amusement, or even church membership, are often discussed by evangelists, and these issues may become conditions of salvation to those who hear. The individual may be willing to accept Christ, but be wholly unable to see beyond that one step until that one step is taken.

Again, a message may become a "false force" and, to some extent, a hindrance in true evangelism, through a common tendency to depend upon it to move the unsaved to decision. Only the Spirit of God can illuminate the vision and convict the heart of its sinfulness; and while the Spirit may use the message to that end, the work is His and His alone.

The divine plan in saving men provides that the Gospel of the saving grace of Christ is to be clearly presented to them. As they hear, some will believe, and when they believe they will that instant be saved by the mighty power of God (John 3:36). There is little demand for methods beyond this God-given program. It is doubtless important to discover and follow up every decision. Simple methods often help to this end; but such machinery is no part of the plan God has ordained. The unsaved are expected to believe the message of salvation as they hear it. Failure is too often in the preaching. The messenger should know the Gospel, or else be silent.

The real purpose of the message and the utter impossibility of its possessing convicting power in and of itself will be more fully stated in another chapter, when dealing with the illuminating work of the Spirit as one of the true forces in the evangelism of the New Testament.

In considering the true forces in evangelism as they are set forth in the Scriptures, it will be found that they, in contrast with the "false forces" already mentioned, depend upon the activity of the whole company of believers in prayer and in the ministry of the Word; that they demand an unceasing effort for their fullest realization; and that they, from necessity, must usually be carried on independently of public gatherings or special leaders. These true forces in evangelism will, for the sake of emphasis, be taken up in their reverse order; beginning with the objective, or end, which true evangelism must have in view, and tracing the successive steps backward to the real point of human responsibility.

Chapter 2

Salvation: The Objective in Evangelism

All evangelism finds its consummation in one phase of the great Scriptural word, "Salvation." It is a word which covers more than the objective of evangelism, in that it includes, beyond the deliverance from the penalty and condemnation of sin, both the deliverance from the present power of sin and the final unfolding and development of the saved one into the image of Christ. The word includes a whole series of other great doctrines and revelations in which the Father, Son, and Holy Spirit are seen working toward the transformation of the individual, body, soul, and spirit, into a celestial being and a partaker with Christ of the heavenly glory. This is the mighty working of the Triune God toward the heavenly perfection of everyone who believes. Blessed indeed are they who learn to yield themselves wholly to His saving power!

Because of the universal Satanic blindness upon the minds of unregenerate people (2 Cor. 4:3, 4) the scope of the transforming work of salvation is not always understood, even where such knowledge is boldly assumed, and many religious leaders, through this blindness, have ignorantly turned away from the real Gospel and have sincerely espoused "another gospel" of social reform, ethical culture, humanitarianism, or morality. In turning to these good but subordinate things they have revealed, both by their careless rejection of the one Gospel of

27

Grace and by their unbounded enthusiasm for these unworthy substitutes, that the riches of the glorious Gospel of Christ have not dawned on them.

This unconscious ignorance of the central truth of the Word of God is one of the mightiest hindrances to evangelism today; for not only are the blinded unable to take a part in real soul-saving work, but they have pleaded for, and to some extent secured, an attitude of tolerance toward their doctrines from many who should be resisting them in defense of the truth.

The spirit of tolerance toward the preaching of "another gospel," instead of the Gospel of Christ, is usually justified by the assuring statement that the Word of God needs no defense, and therefore any controversy with these perverters of the truth would be a needless and aimless warfare. To this it may be replied: No defense of the whole truth is ever made from a fear that man will destroy the eternal Word itself, but that defense is made from a God-given compassion for the multitude who are being beguiled away from all hope by the sophistries of these teachings; for any true burden for the lost will extend to the misguided as much as to the unguided.

With the many pious substitutes for the one Gospel of Grace today, and the ecclesiastical influence and blind enthusiasm of their promoters, evangelism has new enemies to face, and her glorious work can never be accomplished by waving the white flag of tolerance before these foes.

Since much depends, in true evangelism, on a clear understanding of all that is included in "the power of God unto salvation," it is important to dwell at some length on the various aspects of salvation. This is undertaken with a deep consciousness that the heart-comprehension of the glorious riches of salvation must depend upon a divine illumination, or, as it is stated in the Scriptures: "That the God of our Lord Jesus Christ, the Father of glory, may give unto you the spirit of wisdom and revelation in the knowledge of him: the eyes of your understanding being enlightened; that ye may know what is the hope of his calling, and what the riches of the glory of his inheritance in the saints" (Eph. 1:17, 18).

In 1 Cor. 1:30, Christ is set forth as having been made unto the believer, "Righteousness, Sanctification, and Redemption."

These three words, to some extent, suggest the three tenses—past, present, and future—of salvation; for the believer was saved from condemnation unto righteousness and life when he believed; he is being saved from the habit and power of sin through sanctification; and he will be saved from the presence of sin when he, with his glorious body, is wholly redeemed and complete in the presence of his Lord at His Coming.

The present and future tenses of salvation, though in no way a part of evangelism, should be carefully distinguished from the past tense, which is its true objective.

To the believer who has come into the first great tense of salvation, the body of truth mentioned above which sets forth "Sanctification," or "the second tense of salvation," is of greatest import; for it presents to him the only solution of all the problems gathering about his responsibility to walk worthy of the vocation wherewith he is called, and to show forth the virtues of Him Who has called him from darkness into His marvelous light. The believer's high position of sonship with God, co-partnership with Christ, and communion and fellowship with the Spirit of Holiness Who indwells him, demands nothing short of a God-wrought salvation from the habit and power of sin, which is independent of all human energy and strength; for human nature, at its best, has no capacity to produce the smallest part of a true God-honoring life.

It may further be stated in this connection that no intelligent Christian can contemplate the threefold fact of his own high calling in Christ Jesus, his sinful nature, and the overpowering strength of his adversary, Satan, and not welcome the God-provided victory and salvation by the Spirit from the control and domination of evil. It is, however, often difficult for the child of God to abandon his own resources and tendency to self-help as a means to victory, and to rest in faith and expectation toward God that He will work in him both to will and to do of His good pleasure; yet the victory over evil is never gained by any other plan than a complete dependence upon the saving power of God through Jesus Christ. "He which has begun a good work in you will perform it until the day of Jesus Christ" (Phil. 1:6).

So it is revealed that the last tense of salvation, even that faultless presentation before the presence of His glory, is a work which is accomplished independent of all human energy and strength.

In each revealed purpose of God for man in the ages past, some responsibility has fallen upon the faithfulness of man; but in this age of grace, wherein God is calling out a heavenly people, it is as though He would not allow the glorious result to be marred by one human touch, so perfectly has He reserved to Himself, every necessary step in the great work of man's salvation.

Returning to the first tense of salvation, or that which is the real objective in true evangelism, it will be seen that this part of the saving work of God includes the greatest issues that can come into a human life. Some of the more important aspects of the first tense of salvation will here be considered separately:

I. Sins' Penalty

The penalty of sin and the condemnation of an offended law are wholly set aside through justification, and on the grounds of the substitutionary, sacrificial death of Christ. As it is recorded in Eph. 1:7: "In whom we have redemption through his blood, the forgiveness of sins, according to the riches of his grace," and so complete has been this atoning work that God, in perfect justice and righteousness, can not only forgive and cancel all sin, but He can also receive the forgiven sinner as covered with all the worthiness of Christ. The same passage records: "Having predestinated us unto the adoption of children by Jesus Christ to himself, according to the good pleasure of his will, to the praise of the glory of his "grace, wherein he has made us accepted in the beloved" (Eph. 1:5, 6).

This is an atonement based upon substitution. It is the only meaning given in the New Testament to the death of Christ, and it is the only value foreseen in that death in the types and prophecies of the Old Testament. In Isa. 53:5, 6, it is written: "But he was wounded for our transgressions, he was bruised for our iniquities: the chastisement of our peace was upon him; and with his stripes we are healed. All we like sheep have gone astray; we have turned every one to his own way; and the Lord has laid on him the iniquity of us all." To reject this repeated and only revelation of the purpose of God in the cross is to set sail upon a shoreless sea of uncertainty, to abandon the only cure for sin which the world can ever know, and to forsake the one and only foundation, according to God's revelation to man, upon which every hope for humanity is made to rest.

This fact, namely, that the divine compassion fulfilled all the demands of righteousness in behalf of sinful and unrighteous man, stands without any worthy comparison or illustration in the range of human experience. Nevertheless there are interpreters of the meaning of the death of Christ who claim that they find a line of analogy to this great revelation in the things of this world. They claim that such sacrifice is to be seen in the dying of one generation of flowers for the enrichment of future generations of flowers; and that the suffering of a mother for her child is, in principle, akin to the suffering of the cross. The failure of all such comparisons may be seen in the fact that the dying of one generation of flowers does not save any future generations from death; nor does the suffering of a mother substitute, or in any way relieve, the pain and sufferings of the child.

Christ did not die to show us how to die: He died that we might not die. Apart from this central distinction, there may be maintained a "form of religion"; but there can be no power in the salvation thus offered. There may be a carefully selected use of Scripture; but there can be no reasonable interpretation of the whole testimony of God.

The sin question was met and perfectly dealt with by God, He Himself being the sole mediator, and the result is a perfect lifting of all penalty and condemnation for sin. All humanity was included in this mediation; for it is written, "And he is the propitiation for our sins: and not for ours only, but also for the sins of the whole world" (1 John 2:2), and "that he by the grace of God should taste death for every man" (Heb. 2:9), and again, "God so loved the world that he gave his only begotten Son" (John 3:16). Hence it is revealed that the condemnation of the unsaved is not now the sins which Christ bore in His body on the tree; but the condemnation rests in the fact of the rejection of the Sin-bearer. Thus it is written: "He that believeth on him is not condemned: but he that believeth not is condemned already, because he has not believed in the name of the only begotten Son of God." Even so, the Spirit convinces a world that rejects its propitiation, of but one great sin: "Of sin, because they believe not on me."

The believer, in contrast to the unsaved, has consented to the atonement as the basis of his salvation, and has thus appropriated by faith the propitiation made for him.

The exact position of the believer in relation to the condemnation justly due him for his sins may be illustrated by the relation which an executed criminal bears to the law which has already condemned and put him to death. He has been drawn into court, judged and sentenced to death for his sins, and the death penalty has been perfectly executed. His execution has, however, been borne for him, in substitution, by the very Judge Whose righteousness condemned him. For it must ever be remembered that it was the Judge Who pronounced the death sentence—"The soul that sinneth, it shall die," and "The wages of sin is death"—Who also in His great love bowed the heavens and came down from that throne, making bare His own bosom and receiving into His own breast the very death blow he had in righteousness imposed. It was God that "was in Christ, reconciling the world unto himself, not imputing their trespasses unto them."

The believer, thus standing beyond his own perfect execution, is in a position which is not under law; for the last demand of the law has been satisfied. He is in a position, therefore, wherein God is free to work out every desire of His own love without a possible challenge of His perfect righteousness and true holiness. Since all the demands of righteousness have been so fully satisfied, it is written that God can remain just, and still be the justifier of him that believeth. When God is thus free to act He will accomplish by His own power His eternal purpose and the believer will finally be presented faultless before the presence of His glory, and will be conformed to the image of His Son.

Wonderful indeed are the figures used in the Bible to set forth the complete removal of sin and condemnation from the one who receives the God-provided cure for sin. In Micah 7:9 it is said of Israel: "And thou wilt cast all their sins into the depths of the sea"; so also, in Psa. 103:12: "As far as the east is from the west, so far hath he removed our transgressions from us," "And their sins and iniquities will I remember no more" (Heb. 10:17). And again, the strong figure of "blotting out" is frequently used: I, even I, am he that blotteth out thy transgressions for mine own sake, and will not remember thy sins" (Isa. 43:25). "I have blotted out, as a thick cloud, thy transgressions, and, as a cloud, thy sins: return unto me; for I have redeemed thee" (Isa. 44:22). "But those things which God has before showed by the mouth of all his prophets, that Christ should suffer, he has so fulfilled. Repent ye, therefore, and be converted, that your sins may be blotted out" (Acts 3:19).

So again, this forgiveness of sin, as in the passage just quoted, is said to be made possible only in the blood of the cross. In Col. 2:13-14: "And you, being dead in your sins and the uncircumcision of your flesh, has he quickened together with him, having forgiven you all your trespasses; blotting out the handwriting of ordinances that was against us, which was contrary to us, and took it out of the way, nailing it to his cross."

II. *New Clothing Demanded*

Not only is sin and condemnation removed in the first tense of salvation, but the saint, whether of the Old Testament or the New, is said to be "clothed with the righteousness of God" in place of the "filthy rags" of self-righteousness, as the following Scriptures describe: "But we are as an unclean thing, and our righteousness are as filthy rags" (Isa. 64:6). "I will greatly rejoice in the Lord, my soul shall be joyful in my God; for he has clothed me with the garments of his salvation, he has covered me with the robe of righteousness" (Isa. 61:10). "Let thy priests be clothed with righteousness; and let thy saints shout for joy" (Psa. 132:9). The passage, "Unto Adam also and to his wife did the Lord make coats of skins, and clothed them" (Gen. 3:21), is a suggestion of Christ made our righteousness through the shedding of blood.

So, also, many other passages reveal that this imputed righteousness is possible only on the ground of faith in Christ as personal Savior through His sacrificial death: "But now the righteousness of God without the law is manifest, being witnessed by the law and the prophets; even the righteousness of God which is by faith of Jesus Christ unto all and upon all them that believe" (Rom. 3:21, 22). "What shall we say then that Abraham our father, as pertaining to the flesh, has found? For if Abraham were justified by works, he has whereof to glory; but not before God. For what saith the scripture? Abraham believed God, and it was counted unto him for righteousness. Now to him that worketh is the reward not reckoned of grace, but of debt. But to him that worketh not, but believeth on him that justifieth the ungodly, his faith is counted for righteousness. Even as David also describeth the blessedness of the man, unto whom God imputeth righteousness without works" (Rom. 4:1-6). "For they, being ignorant of God's righteousness, and going about to establish their own righteousness, have not submitted themselves unto the righteousness of God. For Christ is the end of the law for righteousness to every one that believeth" (Rom. 10:3, 4). "That I may win Christ, and be found in him, not having my own righteousness, which is of the law, but that which is through the faith of Christ, the righteousness which is of God by faith" (Phil. 3:8, 9). "And to her was granted that she should be arrayed in fine linen, clean and white: for the fine linen is the righteousness of saints" (Rev. 19:8). "But of him are ye in Christ Jesus, who of God was made unto us wisdom from God, and righteousness and sanctification, and redemption" (1 Cor. 1:30, A.V.). "For he has made him to be sin for us, who knew no sin; that we might be made the righteousness of God in him" (2 Cor. 5:21).

Space has been given to these many passages that imputed righteousness may be seen to be, as it is, an important theme in both the Old and New Testaments, and a necessary thing as well, if sinful man is ever to appear before Jehovah God. So also, in these Scriptures of the New Testament this "imputed" righteousness is said to be Christ Himself "made our righteousness" by an act of God; for according to the last passage quoted, the believer is made the righteousness of God in Christ as perfectly as Christ was made sin for him. His position is said to be "in Christ" and he is accepted in the beloved.

There is also a position of perfect justification through the work of the Sin-bearer. "For Christ is the end of the law for righteousness to every one that believeth" (Rom. 10:4). Under these "riches of grace" righteousness is not required; but is rather bestowed as the basis of acceptance before God, and righteousness is fulfilled *in*, rather than *by* the believer.

The revelation that the righteousness of God is "unto all and upon all that believe" has always seemed an impossible and unreasonable thing from the viewpoint of the "wisdom of this world"; but it is not impossible or unreasonable in the light of the cross.

III. The New Life Makes Alive

Also there is in salvation an impartation of a new life; and that which alone can bring relief to one who is "dead in trespasses and sins." It is a new creation and regeneration by the power of God on the grounds of the blood of the cross. It, too, is bestowed at the beginning of salvation.

The following passages, selected from over eighty New Testament references on this theme, will give some conception of the whole doctrine and revelation:

1. *It is in no way the present possession of the unsaved.* "Jesus answered and said unto him, Verily, verily, I say unto thee, Except a man be born again [from above], he cannot see the kingdom of God" (John 3:3). "Verily, verily, I say unto you, Except ye eat the flesh of the Son of man, and drink his blood, ye have no life in you" (John 6:53). "Because strait is the gate, and narrow the way, which leads unto life, and few there be that find it" (Matt. 7:14).

2. *Eternal life is the present possession of the believer.* "Verily, verily, I say unto you, he that heareth my word, and believeth on him that sent me, has everlasting life, and shall not come into condemnation; but is passed from death unto life" (John 5:24). "He that believeth on the Son has everlasting life: and he that believeth not the Son shall not see life; but the wrath of God abideth on him" (John 3:36). "These things have I written unto you that believe on the name of the Son of God; that ye may know that ye have eternal life" (1 John 5:13).

While eternal life is a present possession of the believer and now secure (John 5:24; 10:28), it is, like salvation, referred to a few times in its future aspect: "Be thou faithful unto death and I will give thee the crown of life" (Rev. 2:10). "But godliness is profitable unto all things, having promise of the life that now is, and of that which is to come" (1 Tim. 4:8).

3. *Eternal life is from Christ.* "In him was life; and the life was the light of men" (John 1:4). "Jesus saith unto him, I am the way, the truth, and the life: no man cometh unto the Father, but by me" (John 14:6). "But ye denied the Holy One and the Just, and desired a murderer to be granted unto you; and killed the Prince of life, whom God has raised from the dead; whereof 'we are witnesses'" (Acts 3:14, 15). "This is the record, that God hath given unto us eternal life, and the life is in his Son" (1 John 5:11).

4. *Eternal life is the indwelling Christ* (also spoken of as a divine nature 2 Pet. 1:4; and the "new man" Col. 3:10). "Then Jesus said unto them, Verily, verily, I say unto you; Except ye eat the flesh of the Son of man, and drink his blood, ye have no life in you. Whoso eateth my flesh, and drinketh my blood, hath eternal life; and I will raise him up at the last day. For my flesh is meat indeed, and my blood is drink indeed. He that eateth my flesh, and drinketh my blood, dwelleth in me, and I in him. As the living Father has sent me, and I live by the Father: so he that eateth me, even he shall live by me" (John 6:53-57). "To whom God would make known what is the riches of the glory of this mystery among the Gentiles; which is Christ in you, the hope of glory" (Col. 1:27). "When Christ, who is our life, shall appear, then shall ye also appear with him in glory" (Col. 3:4). "I am crucified with Christ; nevertheless I live; yet not I, but Christ liveth in me: and the life which I now live in the flesh I live by the faith of the Son of God, who loved me, and gave himself for me" (Gal. 2:20). "Examine yourselves, whether ye be in the faith; prove your own selves. Know ye not your own selves, how that Jesus Christ is in you, except ye be reprobates?" (2 Cor. 13:5). "Always bearing about in the body the dying of the Lord Jesus, that the life also of Jesus might be made manifest in our body" (2 Cor. 4:10).

5. *Eternal life is conditioned on faith in Christ as Savior.* "But these are written, that ye might believe that Jesus is the Christ, the Son of God; and that believing ye might have life through his name" (John 20:31). "But as many as received him, to them gave he power to become the sons of God, even to them that believe on his name: which were born, not of blood, nor of the will of the flesh, nor of the will of man, but of God"

(John 1:12, 13). "For the wages of sin is death; but the gift of God is eternal life through Jesus Christ our Lord" (Rom. 6:23).

Thus regeneration is set forth in the Scriptures as a most important part of the work of salvation; and since all its aspects are foreign to the things of this world, it is wholly omitted from other religious systems; and since it is the only gateway through which a soul can be delivered from the power of darkness and translated into the kingdom of God's dear Son (Col. 1:13), it, too, is carefully omitted from the creeds of Satan, and from the teachings of his apostles (2 Cor. 2:13-15). Yet, if this revelation is rejected, what other interpretation can be given to this great body of truth? Or what other dynamic can be substituted that will enable the soul to rise to the present and future estate of the Christian, as that estate is described in the Word of God?

IV. *The Gift of the Spirit*

The God-honoring quality of life in the believer has suffered untold failure through the almost universal confusion and neglect of the truth in regard to the work of the Spirit in and through the believer. This misunderstanding begins even with that part of the Spirit's work in which He prepares a soul for salvation.

In the relation of the Spirit to the believer it is, perhaps, most important to recognize that the Spirit takes up His permanent abode in the believer at the moment he is saved. Receiving the Spirit is not, then, a "second blessing" bestowed upon especially consecrated Christians in answer to believing prayer; for, since the Day of Pentecost, and since the Gospel was given to the Gentiles as recorded in Acts 10, the Spirit has taken His place in the believer at the moment he has passed from death unto life.

In this connection it need only be remembered that in Rom. 5:1-11, where some immediate results of justification by faith are enumerated, it is stated in the fifth verse that "the love of God is shed abroad in our hearts by the Holy Spirit which is given unto us." Also Paul, while correcting the Corinthian Christians for unmentionable sins, based his whole appeal to them on the fact that they were the temples of the Holy Spirit (1 Cor. 6:19). So, also, in Rom. 8:9: "But ye are not in the flesh, but in the Spirit, if so be that the Spirit of God dwell in you. Now if any man have not the Spirit of Christ, he is none of his." And Gal. 4:6: "And because ye are sons, God has sent forth the Spirit of his Son into your hearts, crying, Abba, Father" (see also, John 7:37; 1 Cor. 2:12; 1 John 3:24; 4:13. When rightly understood, Acts 5:34; 8:15-17; 19:1-6, furnish no exception to this positive teaching of God's Word).

It is possible and necessary to be "filled with the Spirit" anew for every time of need (Eph. 5:18); but that should never be confused with receiving the Spirit, which is one of the aspects of the first tense of salvation.

By this new relation to the Spirit, the believer becomes enabled at once to meet all the demands of his new life; both as to its victory over the "old man" with the desires and habits of the flesh, and as to the new undertakings for God of the "new man in all holy living and service which are so infinitely beyond human power and might. The fact that he comes instantly into possession of sufficient power by the Spirit to live wholly unto God is in marked contrast to the world's ideal of "character-building" which demands years of painful defeat and failure. The believer has but to learn to yield himself wholly to the power of the indwelling Spirit to find that he is delivered from all the "works of the flesh" which are these: "Adultery, fornication, uncleanness, lasciviousness, idolatry, witchcraft, hatred, variance, emulations, wrath, strife, seditions, heresies, envyings, murders, drunkenness, revelings, and such like" and in the place of these, the Spirit Who indwells the believer will bear in him "the fruit of the Spirit"; which is "love, joy, peace, long-suffering, gentleness, goodness, faith, meekness, temperance" (Gal. 5:19-24).

Thus the believer, having received the Spirit at the moment he was saved, and being wholly yielded to Him, is enabled from that moment to realize victory over the "old nature," the flesh, and his enemy, Satan. He is able, also, to experience a holy life in fellowship with God; and to find his individual gift of the Spirit for service (Rom. 12:3-8; 1 Cor. 12:4-31); and while there is much sanctifying and teaching work of the Spirit yet to be accomplished in him he may, from the first, fill to the full all the present will of God for him. [1]

---

1. An extended discussion of the work of the Spirit in and through the believer will be found in the author's book, *He That Is Spiritual*.

V. *The Baptism of the Spirit*

Any understanding of this aspect of salvation must depend, in a large measure, upon a clear conception of the various meanings of the word "church" as it is used in the Bible. While that word often refers to a local organization of professing Christians, the word is more often used to designate the whole company of regenerate people who have been, or will be saved during this age of grace. This body of people, or organism, is the true church—"the church which is his body." It is sometimes mentioned directly, and sometimes in types and figures, which suggest the perfect union which exists between Christ and the believers, and between believers themselves. The Shepherd and the sheep (John 10); the Vine and the branches (John 15); the Corner Stone and all the stones of the building (Eph. 2:19-22); the Bridegroom and the bride (Eph. 5:29; 2 Cor. 11:2; Rev. 6:9, with many Old Testament types); the "High Priest" and the "kingdom of priests"; the "Last Adam" and the "new generation"; the Living Head and the one body with its many members (1 Cor. 12:12-31; Eph. 1:22, 23, etc.). The gathering out of this company is the purpose of the present age (Acts 15:13-18); for they are the heavenly people whose purpose and glory will be manifest in all the ages to come.

It is into this body of glorious, heavenly people that the believer is organically placed by the baptism of the Spirit at the moment he is saved. This baptism, by which he is united to his Lord and to his fellow-members in the same body, surpasses all human understanding, and is a union that is closer than any human relationship. The husband and wife are, in the purpose of God, "one flesh"; while it is said of this mystic union of the church with its "Living Head" that they are "one spirit"; "For by one Spirit are we all baptized into one body, whether we be Jews or Gentiles, whether we be bond or free; and have been all made to drink into one Spirit" (1 Cor. 12:13). "He that is joined unto the Lord is one spirit" (1 Cor. 6:17).

So great a relationship must produce some personal experience in the believer, even though this doctrine is wholly unknown by him; hence the test is given for all professing Christians, "We know that we have passed from death unto life, because we love the brethren. He that loveth not his brother [Christian] abideth in death" (1 John 3:4).

The believer's union in the body, as has been stated, is perfect and complete from the very beginning of his saved life; and, while it imposes no demands in personal service beyond his individual responsibility as a believer, it opens before him the blessed certainty of going with that body to meet the Lord when He comes to receive His own (1 Thes. 4:13-19); and to be of the bride, in the bosom of the Bridegroom, in the palace of the King.

VI. *The Christian Priest*

The believer is also constituted a priest unto God when he enters the saved life; he is one of the whole company of priests which is the true church; and he has access, through the blood of the cross, into the holiest place, where Christ, the High Priest, is now entered in. The believer, as a priest in the holiest place, is privileged, like the priest of old, to offer his sacrifice and praise unto God, and to intercede before God for his fellowmen (see 1 Pet. 2:5, 9).

VII. *The Intercession and Advocacy of Christ*

Three times over in the Epistles it is recorded that Jesus now lives to make intercession for believers (Rom. 8:34; Heb. 7:25; 9:24). In addition to this, Christ said in His High Priestly prayer: "I pray for them, I pray not for the world, but for them which thou hast given me; for they are thine" (John 17:9). Thus the unregenerate, when they believe, come instantly into the place of privilege wherein Jesus becomes their Intercessor. This is a vital factor in the safety and security of the one who is resting in Christ by faith; for it is in connection with their keeping that these references to the intercession of Jesus occur. Following the questions, "Who shall lay anything to the charge of God's elect?" and "Who is he that condemneth?" is the assuring answer: "It is Christ that died, yea rather, that is risen again, who is even at the right hand of God, who also maketh intercession for us" (Rom. 8:33, 34). And again: "Wherefore he is able to save them to the uttermost [evermore] that come unto God by him, seeing he ever liveth to make intercession for them" (Heb. 7:25).

Thus Christ, as Intercessor, stands between the weakness and helplessnesss of the saint and the whole requirement of God.

As Advocate, He meets the transgressions and failure of the believer on the ground of His all-sufficient sacrifice for sin. It is written: "My little children, these things write I unto you, that ye sin not. And if any man sin, we have an advocate with the Father, Jesus Christ the righteous" (1 John 2:1, 2). So, to the believer, it is said: "If we confess our sins, he is faithful and just to forgive us our sins, and to cleanse us from all unrighteousness" (1 John 1:9). With the Advocate pleading His own sufficient atonement for the sins of the saved one, the removal of transgression is no longer of present mercy; for God is said to be "faithful and just to forgive us our sins."

Thus Christ has become both the Intercessor and Advocate for the believer; providing him with all cleansing from the defilement of sin and becoming his assurance of security, in spite of his weakness and unworthiness; and all this from the moment he comes "unto God by him." [2]

Any attempt to describe this salvation must prove inadequate; for the half has never been told of the riches of grace in Christ Jesus. Yet enough has been stated to show that the first work in salvation, which is offered to the unregenerate on the grounds of the merit and sacrifice of Christ, is a stupendous and instantaneous transformation of the whole estate of man from the power of darkness and the condemnation of sin, into the glorious light, liberty and security of the sons of God. It is the unmeasured power, wisdom and love of God working, at His own infinite cost, to create a new humanity, redeemed and heavenly in being. Before such an objective the humanitarian substitutes, offered by Satan or man, become as nothing.

This salvation is in no way the product of human thought or invention; but it has rather "appeared" as a "revelation" from God to man (Tit. 3:4, and Gal. 1:11, 12). The awe-inspiring words, "scholars have agreed," is the final evidence offered in defense of other so-called "gospels" of today; but of the one true Gospel

2. A fuller treatment of the revealed truth concerning that which enters into the saving grace of God will be found in the author's book *Salvation*.

of Grace it may be said "all Scripture has agreed," for it is the central message of the Bible from its beginning to its end.

This great salvation is offered to man as a perfect whole and therefore cannot be divided; for there are no divine provisions whereby any portion of this mighty work can be accepted apart from the whole. He who would accept the forgiveness of sin, or a place with the redeemed in glory, can do so only as he accepts the Lord Christ; and with Him, all that God in His infinite love would bestow. And when he is thus saved he will but little comprehend the extent of that redeeming work; yet his limited understanding, while it may deprive him of much joy and blessing, does not change one fact of his new and glorious estate.

Lost men are saved when they believe the offer of this salvation. Salvation is not conditioned upon prayer, repentance, reformation, profession, or "seeking the Lord." Israel sought the Lord while He might be found (Isa. 55:6); but no Gentile "seeketh after God" (Rom. 3:11). "The Son of man is come to seek and to save that which was lost" (Luke 19:10).

It is also clear that the transcendent undertaking of salvation is wholly a work of God, since its every phase depends upon a power that surpasses the whole range of human strength. Because of this, the condition of salvation is reasonable, which demands only an attitude of expectation toward God through Christ. In preparation for this, the blinded and self-sufficient person must not only be so wrought upon that he will want to be saved; but he must see his utter helplessness apart from the power of God and the sacrifice of the cross, and this, in spite of the blinding and opposition of Satan who energizes him (Eph. 2:2).

Who is sufficient for these things? Surely not the eloquent preacher or the pleading evangelist! God alone is sufficient; and He has fully provided for the necessary preparation of mind and heart in the all-important conviction by the Spirit.

Chapter 3

Conviction by the Spirit

Every soul-winner becomes aware, sooner or later, of the fact that the vast company of unsaved people do not realize the seriousness of their lost estate; nor do they become alarmed even when the most direct warning and appeal is given to them. They may be normally intelligent and keen to comprehend any opportunity for personal advancement in material or intellectual things; yet there is over them a spell of indifference and neglect toward the things that would secure for them any right relation to God. All the offers of grace with the present and future blessedness of the redeemed are listened to by these people without a reasonable response. They are, perhaps, sympathetic, warm-hearted and kind; they are full of tenderness toward all human suffering and need; but their sinfulness before God and their imperative need of a Savior are strangely disregarded. They lie down to sleep without fear and awaken to a life that is free from thought or obligation toward God. The faithful minister soon learns, to his sorrow, that his most careful presentation of truth and earnest appeal produces no effect upon them, and the question naturally arises: "How, then, can these people be reached with the Gospel?"

The answer to that question lies in a right understanding of the cause of their indifference, and in an adjustment of methods in work so that there may be co-operation with the Spirit in following the divine program in soul-winning.

One of the greatest foes to modern evangelism, which has

been treated far too lightly, is described in the following passage: "And even if our gospel is veiled, it is veiled in them that are perishing: in whom the God of this age has blinded the thoughts of the unbelieving, that the illumination of the gospel of the glory of Christ, who is the image of God, should not dawn upon them" (2 Cor. 4:3, 4, A.V. with margin).

This passage scarcely needs comment beyond a slight reference to the exact meaning of the word "gospel" as that word is here used.

That body of truth which Paul received as a special revelation (Gal. 1:12), and afterwards called "my gospel," "the gospel of Christ" and "the gospel of God" (Rom. 2:16; Phil. 1:27; 1 Thes. 2:2), is a far more limited theme than the life story of Jesus as recorded in the Four Gospels of the New Testament. It is rather the exact grounds of salvation by the cross of Christ and through the grace of God. It is the whole revelation of the divine propitiation for sin. While this Gospel had a larger mission than the Jew could anticipate, in that it was to be a new revelation from God, and was to be extended to the Gentiles also, it is the divine offer of all of God's provisions for man's salvation in this age; and by it life and immortality were brought to light (2 Tim. 1:10). It is simply the offer of redemption and the statement of those conditions under grace, by which a soul may "turn from darkness unto light and from the power of Satan unto God" (Acts 26:18); and being the point of deliverance "from the power of Satan unto God," it is veiled by Satan and is opposed to all Satanic wisdom and strength. Satan's doctrine (1 Tim. 4:1, 2; Rev. 2:24; cf. 1 Cor. 2:10-12) has always been one of moral perfection secured by self-effort or personal works (Isa. 14:14; Gen. 3:4, 5). His program of self-fitting, resulting only in self-glory, is in complete contrast to the true principle of saving faith, through which one depends on God alone for all needed transformation (Rom. 8:29; 1 John 3:2).

True to this revealed fact of Satanic blindness, we find unregenerate men unable to conceive of any relation to God other than that based on the merit of their own self-made character (John 3:1-8; 1 Cor. 2:1-16). They do not comprehend that "Christ has become the end of the law for righteousness to every one that believeth," and that it is only Satanic blindness which leads them, to "go about to establish their own righteousness" rather than to come under the bestowed righteousness of God (Rom. 3:21, 22; 4:1-6; 10:3, 4; Phil. 3: 8,9; 1 Cor. 1:30; 2 Cor. 5:21).

Saving faith may thus be defined as a voluntary turning from all hope and grounds based on self merit, and assuming an attitude of expectancy toward God, trusting Him to do a perfect saving work based only on the merit of Christ. Such an attitude of anticipation toward God alone is reasonable in the light of the fact that salvation is a divine creative act, and therefore, humanly impossible. But the reasonableness of the case is of no force to one whose reason is blinded at this vital point. It is this solemn fact that evangelism must face. A divine illumination is demanded. No human power or argument is sufficient to enlighten a darkened soul concerning the necessary steps into the way of life. This is a part of the work assigned alone to the all-sufficient Spirit.

It is clear from the Scriptures that the Gospel of the substitutionary sacrifice of Christ is the only possible ground of salvation and escape from "the power of Satan unto God." It is therefore suggestive that Satan is imposing his blindness upon the unregenerate mind only at this one point. The demons in the days of Christ's earthly ministry bore faithful testimony to His deity as the Son of God; just so, Satan is now directly witnessing to the value of the only offers of salvation by thus centralizing all his blinding power upon the way of the cross.

In addition to the exercise of his own power in directly blinding the unsaved as to the value of the cross, Satan is increasingly active, through his ministers, in attempting to exclude this central truth from the Christian faith. To do this he is now, as predicted, forcing great counterfeit religious systems and restatements of doctrine upon the world. It is also suggestive that in all these the only revealed basis of salvation is carefully omitted.

The blinding or veiling of the mind, mentioned in 2 Cor. 4:3, 4, causes a universal incapacity to comprehend the way of salvation, and is imposed upon unregenerate man by the arch enemy of God in his attempts to hinder the purpose of God in redemption. It is a condition of mind against which man can have no power. Yet God has provided a means whereby this

Satanic veil may be lifted, the eyes opened (Acts 26:18), the eyes of the heart enlightened (Eph. 1:18, A.V.), and the soul come into the illumination of the Gospel of the glory of Christ. Then, after this "opening of the eyes" is accomplished, the way of life, which is the Gospel, will seem to the enlightened person to be both desirable and of transcendent import. This great work is accomplished by divine energy, and is one of the mightiest movements of the "power of God unto salvation." It is spoken of in the Scriptures as the drawing of God and the convicting of the Spirit: "No man can come unto me, except the Father which has sent me draw him" (John 6:44). "And when he [the Spirit] is come, he will reprove the world of sin, and of righteousness, and of judgment" (John 16:8).

This individual and particular drawing and reproving should be distinguished from the universal drawing and illuminating of all men that is mentioned in other passages: "And I, if I be lifted up from the earth, will draw all men unto me" (John 12:32), and "That was the true Light which lighteth every man that cometh into the world" (or, "That was the true Light which coming into the world, shineth for every man")—John 1:9. The former passages refer to a special divine work to be accomplished in each individual, and they present the only sufficient means by which a Satan-ruled soul (Eph. 2:2) may be inclined unto God, and by which Satan-blinded eyes may receive a new vision of the Gospel of Grace.

This divine unveiling of the individual mind and heart to the Gospel is spoken of at length in Heb. 6:4-9. While this passage is Jewish in its character, it is an important statement of a phase of the truth under present consideration. The passage is as follows: "For it is impossible for those who were once enlightened, and have tasted of the heavenly gift, and were made partakers of the Holy Ghost, and have tasted the good word of God, and the powers of the world to come, if they shall fall away, to renew them again unto repentance; seeing they crucify to themselves the Son of God afresh, and put him to an open shame. For the earth which drinketh in the rain that cometh oft upon it, and bringeth forth herbs meet for them by whom it is dressed, receiveth blessing from God: but that which beareth thorns and briers is rejected, and is nigh unto cursing; whose end is to be burned. But, beloved, we are persuaded better things of you, and things that accompany salvation, though we thus speak."

It would seem impossible that so much could be accomplished in any person as is here described, and yet that person remain unsaved, were it not for the phase of truth which is under consideration; for the passage states that those described have been "once enlightened," "have tasted of the heavenly gift," and have been made "partakers of the Holy Ghost." They have "tasted the good word of God" and the "powers of the world to come"; yet this is all true of unregenerate persons who have been "drawn" and "convicted" by divine power in preparation for salvation.

When the passage has been interpreted as being a description of regenerate people, it has been used as a proof text to substantiate that unscriptural and God-dishonoring theory that a saved person can "fall away" and find it impossible to renew his repentance. That the passage does not describe a true child of God is evident, for the description is wholly inadequate of a Christian. All that is said is, in a sense, true of a believer; but very much more is true of him also. The believer has *received*, not just "tasted," the heavenly gift; he has been "sealed by the Holy Spirit," which is more than to have "partaken" of the Spirit in conviction or illumination. The "tasting of the Word of God" is a poor substitute for the believer's washing of regeneration by the Word; and "tasting" of the powers of the world to come is incomparable with the power of God in salvation.

But again, it is clearly stated in the closing verse of this passage that this is not a description of the "better things" that "accompany salvation." It is therefore a description of the condition into which a soul is brought when divinely prepared for an intelligent choice of Christ as Savior. This condition is, to some extent, a sphere of probation (which is never the relation of a true beliver to God) for, as the life-giving rain waters the earth and causes it to yield herbs or thorns, so the soul that has been thus favored with the vision of life and salvation in preparation for yielding to the saving power of Christ, may "bear thorns and briers" by continually resisting the vision, and finally "fall away" and find no place for repentance; seeing he crucifies to himself the Son of God afresh and puts Him, to an open shame. While he is rejecting God's best gift and his only hope, there remains no more "a place of repentance." "If therefore, the light that is in thee be darkness, how great is that darkness."

The importance of this truth will warrant a reference to three other brief passages. In each of these this divine drawing, or calling, may be seen in its true place and order among the other aspects of "the power of God unto salvation." In these passages, this phase of truth is mentioned by the words, "to open their eyes," "called me by His grace," and "called." The passage reads:

"To open their eyes, and to turn them from darkness to light, and from the power of Satan unto God, that they may receive forgiveness of sins, and inheritance among them which are sanctified by faith that is in me" (Acts 26:18). "But when it pleased God, who separated me from my mother's womb, and called me by his grace, to reveal his Son in me, that I might preach him among the heathen; immediately I conferred not with flesh and blood" (Gal. 1:15, 16). "Moreover, whom he did predestinate, them, he also called: and whom he called, them he also justified: and whom he justified, them he also glorified" (Rom. 8:30).

Other passages which emphasize the necessary illumination of the Spirit should also be quoted: "No man can come to me, except the Father which has sent me draw him: and I will raise him up at the last day. It is written in the prophets, And they shall be all taught of God. Every man therefore that has heard, and hath learned of the Father, cometh unto me" (John 6:44, 45). "Wherefore I give you to understand, that no man speaking by the Spirit of God calleth Jesus accursed: and that no man can say that Jesus is Lord, but by the Holy Ghost" (1 Cor. 12:3). "He saith unto them: But whom say ye that I am? And Simon Peter answered and said, Thou art the Christ, the Son of the living God. And Jesus answered and said unto him, Blessed art thou, Simon Bar-jona: for flesh and blood hath not revealed it unto thee, but my Father which is in heaven" (Matt. 16:15-17).

This special aspect of the divine work, which has been seen in these passages already quoted, is more particularly dwelt upon in John 16:8-11. The whole context of this passage (16:8-15) announces, in addition to the threefold work of the Spirit for the unsaved, or "world," a special instructive and illuminative work of the Spirit for the saved, here addressed as "you." As these two classes were distinguished in connection with a previously quoted Scripture, their difference should be noted here also. In this connection it will be seen that the saved are to be led into "all truth"; while the unsaved are to be instructed along but one particular line. To the saved the "all things" of Christ and of God are to be shown; while the unsaved are to see only that which first concerns them, which is the way of life in Christ Jesus. This passage referring to the work of the Spirit for the unsaved is as follows: "Nevertheless I tell you the truth; it is expedient for you that I go away: for if I go not away, the Comforter will not come unto you; but if I depart, I will send him unto you. And when he is come, he will reprove the world of sin, and of righteousness, and of judgment: of sin, because they believe not on me; of righteousness, because I go to my Father, and ye see me no more; of judgment, because the prince of this world is judged" (John 16:7-11).

In considering this passage it may first be noted that the word "reprove" (R.V. "convict") is not limited, as is often supposed, to the first word "sin," but applies to the words "righteousness" and "judgment" as well. This suggests a much larger meaning to the word than an acute mental agony for sin, though that might follow. The word "reprove," as here used, suggests a process of illumination concerning three distinct facts, rather than the creation of a feeling of remorse for sins that have been committed. There is no warrant for assuming that this threefold divinely wrought vision is divisible, or in any way subject to a partial fulfillment. It would, therefore, be unreasonable to limit our thought of this ministry of the Spirit to any one aspect of this work.

A careful study of, in all, about sixteen passages where the Greek word translated "reprove "is used will reveal that it is usually descriptive of a condition of mind resulting from the impartation of truth, and that this convicting work of the Spirit for the world is identical with the enlightenment by the Spirit already considered.

At this point much depends upon an adequate understanding of the whole scope of the action of the Spirit as suggested by the three words, "sin," "righteousness" and "judgment."

Of Sin, "because they believe not on me." "Jesus answered and said unto him, Verily, verily, I say unto thee, Except a man be born again, he cannot see the kingdom of God" (John 3:3). "But the natural man receiveth not the things of the Spirit of God: for they are foolishness unto him: neither can he know them, because they are spiritually discerned" (1 Cor. 2:14).

It is just this incapacity and blindness of the unregenerate mind which is stated in these passages that demands the illuminating work of the Spirit in "convincing of sin." It is evident from the words "because they believe not on me" that they do not comprehend the way of life in Christ Jesus, nor has the light of the glorious Gospel of Christ dawned on them. The only sin to be revealed, according to this passage, is the sin of personally rejecting Christ (see also John 3:18). The reason that there is but one sin is obvious. Christ has perfectly borne the condemnation of the individual's sins, hence God in no wise lays them back again upon the sinner; but rather holds him responsible for not believing the record of the atoning death of His Son (1 John 5:10-12). Hence it is clear that present condemnation cannot result from the sins which God reckons to be covered by the blood of His Son. The issue is plainly the rejection of the Son Who bore the sins. The fact that the blinded sinner must comprehend that his sins have been borne for him by Christ, and that he has the one responsibility of receiving that Savior and his saving work, however, demands a further illumination by the Spirit.

The Gospel demands a special revelation for its understanding; since it announces to all humanity a perfect freedom from the penalty of sin, and also presents the corresponding fact that there can be but one reason for condemnation; and that, the rejection of the Savior, Who bore the sin. Man's relation to God on the question of sin, in the light of the cross, is so unnatural to the unregenerate mind, and is so much the object of Satanic blinding that there can be no understanding of this truth apart from a direct and personal illumination by the Spirit.

The work of the Spirit, it will thus be seen, is to reveal the cure of sin as already accomplished, and to warn against the only remaining possible condemnation that must follow the rejection of the cross. Though the unsaved, "natural man," may be educated, gentle, refined, or gifted, he has no vision of salvation, and thus it is obvious that there can be no adequate conception of the one condemning sin of rejecting Christ as Savior, until the Christ and His saving work as sin-bearer are made real. This the Spirit accomplishes by convincing of righteousness and judgment; for both the conviction of righteousness and of judgment are but revelations of the Christ and His salvation.

Of Righteousness, "because I go to my Father and ye see me no more." "But ye denied the Holy One and the Just, and desired a murderer to be granted unto you; and killed the Prince of life, whom God has raised from the dead; whereof we are witnesses" (Acts 3:14, 15). "Who was delivered for our offenses, and was raised again for our justification" (Rom. 4:5).

In the vision of the Righteous One Who died upon the cross it will be revealed to the unsaved by the Spirit that "God was in Christ reconciling the world unto himself," and that He, the Righteous One, bore the curse of the sinner's unrighteousness "in his own body on the tree." That it was the Righteous One Who died is forever assured by His resurrection and present place in glory. This is the all-important vision; for the Righteous One upon the cross is the sinner's only point of contact with the saving power of God. In like manner, also, as the ground work of salvation is revealed by the convicting work of the Spirit to be the death of the Righteous One, so the enjoyment of all present blessing in fellowship and security must depend upon a direct and personal revelation by the Spirit of the present living Christ.

The problem of all human destiny is the attainment unto the righteousness of God; for without that perfection man can never hope to stand in the presence of God (Heb. 12:10, 14). Christ was made sin for us, He Who knew no sin, that we might be made righteousness of God in Him. He, the Righteous One, bore our sins in His death, and thereby satisfied all the demands of the Father. The Christ in the flesh lived and fulfilled every requirement of God's law, and offered Himself a perfect sacrifice for imperfect humanity. In Him Who became visible, died, rose, ascended and is now invisible, but still the living Lord, "God blessed forever," the sinner is made "accepted in the beloved," and stands in the righteousness of God. This position of being clothed in the righteousness of God through the merit and Person of the living Christ must be recognized as wholly due to the fact that He was really made to be sin for us.

Hence, in convincing of righteousness, the vision is created in the unregenerate mind of the Righteous One Who died on the cross as a personal Savior Who is now raised from the dead, and seated in glory with all His atoning work accepted before God, and Who is able to "guard that which is committed unto him against that day." On the cross Christ judged all sin and secured a perfect salvation for all who believe. So in heaven He saves those who have believed from every challenge of a broken law. Christ is "made unto us righteousness." It is rest to a sin-conscious soul to know that there is a perfect righteousness for him in Christ. Such knowledge cannot be gained apart from the illuminating work of the Spirit.

Of Judgment, "because the prince of this world is judged." "Now is the judgment of this world: now shall the prince of this world be cast out" (John 12:31). "And you, being dead in your sins and the uncircumcision of your flesh, has he quickened together with him, having forgiven you all trespasses; blotting out the handwriting of ordinances that was against us, which was contrary to us, and took it out of the way, nailing it to his cross; and having spoiled principalities and powers, he made a show of them openly, triumphing over them in it" (Col. 2:13-15).

The Spirit thus also enlightens the darkened mind concerning the complete and sufficient judgment of all sin in the cross of Christ. This judgment not only met all possible condemnation for sin (Isa. 53:4-6; Rom. 6:10; 2 Cor. 5:14, 21; Heb. 10:2-18; 1 Pet. 1:18, 19; 2:24), but broke all claim and authority of the rulers and powers of darkness (Col. 2:13-15). Through the dying Christ it is possible to be forever delivered out of Satan's darkness (Col. 1:12-14), and through the living Christ it is promised that the child of God shall be forever saved and kept unto the "Kingdom of God's dear Son" (Rom. 5:10). This is the plan of God's redeeming grace, and it may be concluded, in all confidence, that as certainly as Satan is blinding the minds of the unregenerate men at the point of the redemptive work of Christ, so certainly it is the purpose of God that the Spirit shall unveil their minds concerning that same truth.

The claim which Satan held upon man, before the cross, was the very fact of man's sin and unlikeness to God. That claim was wholly broken by the cross, and the curse of sin was lifted for all. Since the cross, it has been Satan's one advantage to blind those in his power as to the fact of the universal atonement for sin, and to secure an attitude of misunderstanding and rejection of this atonement that will keep man under the last and only condemnation: "that they believe not on me."

Thus all "principalities and powers" were "spoiled" and "triumphed over" in the divine judgment of sin. Now the way of redemption is open to all who will come by the cross. But it is this very value of the death of Christ that is the object of Satan's blinding, and the Spirit alone can unveil the blinded unregenerate mind. This He does by convincing of the perfect judgment for all men now accomplished through the cross.

It cannot be emphasized too strongly that the phase of the Gospel which Satan has veiled from "those that are perishing" is the way of life through the death of Christ, and that it is the same central truth which the Spirit would make real to "those that are perishing," by convincing them "of sin, of righteousness and of judgment."

In this connection it is not claimed that an unsaved person must come to know every phase of truth about the atonement of Christ before he is divinely prepared for salvation; but it is claimed that the Spirit proposes to make the meaning of the cross sufficiently clear to that person as to enable him to abandon all hope of self-worlds, and to turn to the finished work of Christ alone in intelligent, saving faith. The unfolding of redemptive truth was revealed to Paul directly from God, and there is a very real sense in which that truth must be directly revealed to every individual, that he may himself choose it as the only basis of his hope. The atoning sacrificial death of Christ as a distinct and sufficient foundation for salvation must become a reality before it can become a finality in saving faith.

And in convincing the world of sin, righteousness, and of judgment that truth is made real by the Spirit.

What human argument or influence can convince Satan-blinded minds that to fail to believe on Jesus Christ is the all-condemning sin? Surely that sin will not be seen in all its magnitude until the mind has been enlightened in regard to the Person of Christ and His atoning work. Thus only by the Spirit can any conception be had of all that is being rejected when they "believe not on me."

No understanding of the illuminating work of the Spirit on the minds of the unsaved would be complete apart from the recognition of the important agency or means used by the Spirit in that work.

The Word of God, "which is the sword of the Spirit." Another sharp distinction must be made at this point, as in the enlightening and teaching work of the Spirit, between the whole divine work for the saved and that small part of the same work which may be done for the unsaved as a preparation for salvation. The riches of the work for the saved can be only suggested here.

To the saved the Word of God is a cleansing, sanctifying and reflecting power (John 13:10, 11; 15:3; Eph. 5:25, 26; John 17:17; and 2 Cor. 3:18).

To the unsaved, the Word of God is the "sword of the Spirit" (Eph. 6:17). All those who urge methods in personal work properly lay great stress on the right use of Scripture when dealing with the unsaved. God uses the "Sword of the Spirit," and He has not promised to use anything else in unveiling the blinded mind.

As has been seen, the convicting work of the Spirit involves a radical change in the deepest part of man's being, where his motives and desires are first formed; so that an entirely new conception of the God-provided grounds of redemption and a vision of the glorious Person of Christ are created. As both the Person and the work of Christ are presented in the Scriptures, it is only necessary for the Spirit to vitalize His own Word, either upon the printed page, or through the lips of His messenger, to bring a new light and possibility into the hitherto blinded mind. It is, therefore, said of the Word of God: "For the word of God is quick, and powerful [living and active, A.V.], and sharper than any twoedged sword, piercing even to the dividing asunder of soul and spirit, and of the joints and marrow, and is a discerner of the thoughts and intents of the heart" (Heb. 4:12). The Word itself is, however, but the sword, and must be wielded by the Spirit to be effective.

The fact that the Word of God, in the hands of the Spirit, is living and operative is the only warrant for any appeal to the unsaved; and is a warning, as well, that the message, to be effective, must be in accord with the whole truth of God that it may be used by the Spirit. It is a conspicuous fact that every successful soul-winner has been a fearless defender of every essential doctrine of the Scriptures.

The skill of the evangelist, or the pastor who would do the work of an evangelist, is manifested in the ability to present the particular body of redemptive truth repeatedly, yet with freshness and variety.

The evangelist is limited to that evangel which unfolds the cure of sin and the way of life by the substitutionary death of Christ, since that is the only message which the Spirit can use as His Sword in unveiling those eyes which are blinded to that particular truth. How helpless, then, in true soul-saving cooperation with God is that person who has a heart of unbelief toward the blood of Christ, or whose message has been beguiled away from the way of life in Christ Jesus, to an appeal for morality or religious ceremonials, which are the result of human energy and expediencies!

Jesus has commanded His own that are in the world to preach the Gospel of redemptive truth to every creature; yet their preaching is of no avail save as it is accompanied by the convincing and illuminating work of the Spirit, and this work of the Spirit is dependent upon a ministry of the believer which should always accompany preaching. This ministry is the prayer of intercession.

Thus it may be concluded on the question of the use of the Word in true evangelism that it is the work of the Spirit to present the sacrificial judgment of the cross and the living glorious Person of Christ to the unsaved through the preaching of the Word. And when a preacher evades either the message of the cross or the essential deity of Christ there has been, and can be, no co-operation of the Spirit in convincing power, though every element of literary merit and human eloquence be supplied. Evidence of this is on every hand.

It is not a mere arbitrary caprice with God that there must be an intelligent appropriation of the work of Christ as the grounds of redemption: "For there is none other name under heaven given among men, whereby we must be saved" (Acts 4:12). On no other grounds can the mercy and grace of God be exercised in righteousness and justice. It follows, therefore, that the grounds of redemption must be sufficiently clear to each individual to elicit a repose of faith, and a willing deposit of all eternal interests into the saving power of Christ. No human argument or teaching can dispel the Satanic darkness which hinders saving faith, or create the new vision that is required. It is quite possible for a blinded soul to be religious, or even to pose as a minister of the Gospel; yet, having never comprehended the way of life, to be "tossed to and fro by every wind of doctrine," and, though sincere, and possessing a wide range of human knowledge, to be in his blindness only the minister of Satan (2 Cor. 11:13-15).

The wide difference in appreciation of the Gospel which exists between people of equal mental attainments cannot be explained on the grounds of personal temperament or training, else their various attitudes would be more or less permanent, when in reality the attitude of indifference is often suddenly changed to a glowing fire. It need hardly be pointed out that unsaved men do not weigh the evidence of testimony and fact as accurately in matters relating to salvation as they do in any other sphere of investigation. In matters between men in the world the sworn testimony of two reliable witnesses demands a corresponding conclusion; yet the obvious fact of regeneration and the willing testimony of multitudes, "whereas I was blind, now I see," creates little impression on others who are yet in their blindness.

There is a reality in Satanic blindness. But, blessed be God, there is a reality in divine illumination!

It should be observed that, apart from the power of God, superficial decisions may easily be secured, and apparently great results accomplished; for some minds are so dependent upon the opinions of others that the earnest and dominating appeal of the evangelist, with the obvious value of a religious life, is sufficient to move them to follow almost any plan that is made to appear to be expedient. They may be urged to act on the vision of the way of life which the preacher possesses, when they have received no sufficient vision for themselves. The experience of thousands of churches has proven that such decisions have not met the conditions of grace in "believing with the heart"; for the multitude of advertised converts have often failed, and these churches have had to face the problem of dealing with a class of disinterested people who possess no new dynamic, nor any of the blessings of the truly regenerate life.

It is possible reverently to repeat the most pious phrases and assume devotional attitudes and yet have the inner life in no way correspondingly moved. All such exercise, though producing apparent results, is of no avail in real salvation; for the Spirit has not wrought in such a mind to the end that the utterance of such phrases become the expression of the greatest crisis of the inner life, and the only adequate relief for that soul's sense of utter helplessness and burning thirst for the water of life.

A few genuine decisions may occur among the many, and these have always justified the wholesale evangelizing method. There is, however, a very grave harm done to any who are thus superficially affected, and this harm might sometimes outweigh the good that is done. In reply to this it is argued that nothing can outweigh the value of one soul that is saved; yet when the harm of a false decision is analyzed, it will be seen that the after-state of bewilderment and discouragement which results in an attitude that is almost unapproachable and hopeless, has its unmeasured results as well.

The Gospel will always prove, in this age, "a savor of death unto death" as well as of "life unto life"; for some, even upon whom the Spirit has wrought in conviction, will reject the way of life. But there is no expectation in the evangelism of the Scriptures that souls are to be hurried into unrealities and be misguided in their blindness. In the ministry of the Spirit Who

came to convict the world of sin, of righteousness, and of judgment, God has faithfully provided the one all-sufficient preparation for a full and intelligent decision.

Placing saving trust in the Lord Jesus Christ is an act so
definite that the experience must be abiding. A consciousness
that this step has been taken will naturally remain. Well may
we question our own salvation when uncertain at this point. "I
know whom I have believed" is the normal testimony of every
saved person. Such trust abides. It is a consciousness that He
alone is depended upon as the answer before God for every
problem of a sin-cursed soul. This abiding confidence can be
formed in the heart only through the illuminating, regenerat-
ing, and indwelling work of the Spirit.

The examples of soul-winning in the New Testament present
a conspicuous contrast to some examples of present-day evangelism. So far as the divine record shows there seemed to be
little urging or coaxing, nor was any person dealt with individ-
ually who had not first given evidence of a divinely wrought
sense of need. It is recorded that Peter directed the converts at
Pentecost in the way of life after they were "pricked in their
heart, and said unto Peter and to the rest of the apostles, Men
and brethren, what shall we do"? So also there is no record that
Paul and Silas pleaded with the Philippian jailor to become a
Christian before he had any such desire; but rather, after a
great change had taken place in his whole attitude which com-
pelled him to fall tremblingly before them and say, "Sirs, what
must I do to be saved?" did they personally direct him to "believe on the Lord Jesus Christ." Peter does not send for Cornelius—Cornelius reaches out for Peter. And Saul is led into the
light almost without human aid or direction.

In view of this all-important divine preparation for salvation, it is clear that all evangelism, be it public ministry or
personal work, which does not wait for the movings of the
Spirit in the hearts of the unsaved is insomuch removed from
true co-operation with God, and is in danger of hindering souls.

Such a waiting *on* God and *for* God as is necessary for true
co-operation with the Spirit, although it may shatter the evangelist's claim to large numbers of converts, will tend to wean
the church away from her dependence upon spasmodic peri-

ods of concern for the lost into a true and more constant attitude of fruit-bearing.

The Scriptures furnish us with examples of true evangelism, the results of which were reported many centuries ago when it was said: "And the Lord added to the church daily such as should be saved" (Acts 2:47). This blessed condition will always result when believers depend upon the Lord to add to the Church and they continue "steadfastly in the apostles' doctrine and fellowship, and in breaking of bread, and in prayers" (Acts 2:2).

Chapter 4

The Prayer of Intercession

In this attempt to consider the successive aspects of the movements of the "power of God unto salvation," it has already been seen that true evangelism must face the humanly impossible task of lifting the Satanic veil that rests upon all unregenerate minds in connection with the one subject, "the Gospel." This blinding by Satan having been imposed at this one point, for the sufficient reason that "the Gospel" is the revelation of the only way of escape for sinful man from the power of Satan unto God, both the "good news" of the finished work upon the cross and the glory of the living Christ in His present position as Intercessor and Advocate, have been obscured. On the other hand, it has been seen that there is a divinely provided illumination by the Spirit which causes the same "good news" of the finished work and the present glory of Christ to become a reality to the hitherto blinded mind.

The unveiling of the Gospel by the Spirit is necessary and reasonable. For the conditions of saving faith are no less than a deposit of the whole being into the saving power of Christ; and, while superficial decisions may be secured through mere human influence and power, there will be no complete repose of faith until the way is made plain by the enlightenment of the Spirit.

It is true that no man can know the Father, in soul rest, save the Son, and he to whomsoever the Son will reveal Him (Matt. 11:27, 28). This is the basis of all fellowship with God. It is equally true of the unsaved that no man can come to Christ as Savior except the Father draw him (John 6:4). Again, "It is written in the prophets, And they shall be all taught of God. Every man therefore that hath heard, and hath learned of the Father, cometh unto me" (John 6:45).

In view of the appalling absence of personal concern on the part of the multitude of unsaved, in spite of much faithful preaching and exhortation, every serious soul-winner will, sooner or later, raise the question: "What, then, hinders the Spirit from performing His office work of convincing the world of sin, and of righteousness, and of judgment?" The answer to this central question in modern evangelism is found in that subject which is the next step in the successive aspects of the power of God unto salvation, as they are here being considered in their reverse order. That subject is the *Prayer of Intercession*.

There are but three possible ways in which the believer can fulfill the God-appointed human part in seeking the lost. These are: prayer, personal effort or influence, and giving. Both the first and the last are world-wide in their scope, while the other is limited to the locality and opportunity of the individual. There can never be a question as to the relative value of these various lines of service, for the ministry of prayer is continually open to every believer, and is only limited in its possibilities by the feeble faith of man. There is much in the New Testament that emphasizes the importance of preaching the Word as a means unto salvation; but it is evident that there must be more than the human statement of the truth. The Spirit must wield His mighty Sword and that work of the Spirit, to a large extent it would seem, is subject to believing prayer.

A Christian, as has been mentioned in a previous chapter, is, from the moment of his salvation, constituted a royal priest unto God. The meaning and scope of his position may be better understood by referring to the Aaronic priesthood under the Law, for the Old Testament priesthood is evidently a type, or a foreshadowing in some particulars, of the royal priesthood under grace.

That there is a royal priesthood under grace is revealed in the following Scriptures: "But ye are a chosen generation, a royal priesthood, an holy nation, a peculiar people; that ye should show forth the praises [virtues] of him who hath called you out of darkness into his marvelous light" (1 Pet. 2:9). "Ye also, as lively stones, are built up a spiritual house, an holy priesthood, to offer up spiritual sacrifices, acceptable to God by Jesus Christ" (1 Pet. 2:5). "And hath made us kings and priests unto God and his Father; to him be glory and dominion for ever and ever" (Rev. 1:6). "Likewise the Spirit also helpeth our infirmities: for we know not what we should pray for as we ought: but the Spirit itself maketh intercession for us with groanings which cannot be uttered. And he that searcheth the hearts knoweth what is the mind of the Spirit, because he maketh intercession for the saints according to the will of God" (Rom. 8:20, 27).

The essential truth concerning the priesthood under grace is suggested in these passages. Here the priesthood is seen as composed of the members of the body of Christ, which is His Church. A "chosen generation" speaks of their position by the new birth; a "royal priesthood" and "kings and priests" of their office; a "holy nation" and a "holy priesthood" of their necessary cleansing; and a "peculiar people" of their essential heavenly character, as distinguished from the people of the world. So again, "lively stones" speaks of their individual responsibility and service; "offer spiritual sacrifices" and the "intercession by the Spirit" speak of their ministry; while the words "acceptable to God by Jesus Christ" speak of the rent veil, their access to God, and of their "boldness to enter into the holiest by the blood of Jesus, by a new and living way, which he hath consecrated for us, through the veil, that is to say, his flesh" (Heb. 10:19, 20).

Returning to these important teachings to consider them in the same order, and more at length, it will be seen:

I. A "Chosen Generation."

Like the Aaronic priest under the law, the New Testament priest is born to his position. He is constituted a priest unto God as a part of the salvation that is in Jesus Christ. His position and his privileges, therefore, begin with his new birth into the nature and family of God. It is most important to emphasize the truth that every believer is a priest unto God, though he may never intelligently exercise his glorious privilege. The full realization of this position, so far as it affects prayer, is one of the greatest needs among believers today. It is more than a belief in the general efficacy of prayer. It is to be able to say, "I believe God will do His greatest works solely in answer to my prayer."

II. A "Royal Priesthood" and "Kings and Priests."

The New Testament priesthood is an office. This is in marked contrast to the believer's gifts for service. The contrast is seen in the fact that those things which constitute the ministry of the priest are the privilege and duty of all believers alike while the gifts for service are bestowed by the Spirit "as he will" (Rom. 12:3-8; 1 Cor. 12:4-11). Not all believers have the same gift for service; but all are privileged to minister in the priestly office. Not all have the gift of teaching, or of healing; but all have access in prayer.

III. A "Holy Nation" and a "Holy Priesthood."

The importance of cleansing for the exercise of the priestly office under grace is seen through the words "a holy priesthood." It is seen both as it is foreshadowed in the demands for laving and purification of the Old Testament priest, and in the fact that the ministry of the New Testament priest is also in the holiest place, and is directed unto God. In that holy place the least taint of sin or defilement cannot be allowed, though a degree of unfitness might not hinder the exercise of gifts where the service is only to men.

IV. A "Peculiar People."

No greater evidence of the mighty transformation that is wrought by salvation can be found than the fact that the privilege is granted to the one who is saved of entering the holiest place where Christ is already entered in, and is there making intercession for His own who are in the world. Only those who have partaken of the divine nature by regeneration and have come, by grace, to be heavenly in being and destiny could be so favored.

V. "Lively Stones."

As the ministry of gifts in the church is individual, even world-wide evangelism being committed to each believer rather than to the Church as a body, so there is no present service for the New Testament priests as a whole; but their service is individual, as their cleansing and fitness must be.

VI. To "Offer Spiritual Sacrifices" and the "Intercession by the Spirit."

The Old Testament priest was sanctified and cleansed that he might offer sacrifices and enter the "Holy of holies" to intercede for others; so the New Testament priest is appointed to offer sacrifices in three particulars: (a) His own body: "I beseech you, therefore, brethren, by the mercies of God, that ye present your bodies a living sacrifice, holy, acceptable to God, which is your spiritual worship" (Rom. 7:1, R.V., with margin. See also Phil. 2:17; 2 Tim. 4:6; James 1:27). (b) His worship: "By him therefore let us offer the sacrifice of praise to God continually, that is, the fruit of our lips giving thanks to his name" (Heb. 13:15). (c) His substance: "But to do good and to communicate forget not: for with such sacrifices God is well pleased" (Heb. 13:16); "But I have all, and abound: I am full, having received of Epaphroditus the things which were sent from you, an odor of a sweet smell, a sacrifice acceptable, well pleasing to God" (Phil. 4:18). These spiritual sacrifices we may now offer to God.

The New Testament priest is also an intercessor, which, as the word implies, differs from a supplicator who may pray wholly for himself. The intercessor bears the burden and need of others before God, and intercedes in their behalf. No human wisdom is sufficient for this ministry in the holiest place; for "we know not what to pray for as we ought"; but God has anticipated our inability and provided the energizing Spirit Who "maketh intercession for us," and "according to the will of God" (Rom. 8:26, 27).

VII. "Acceptable unto God by Jesus Christ."

How much is required in those searching words, "acceptable to God"! Yet how perfect is the believer's fitting "by Jesus Christ"! Only some personal defilement uncleansed, or sin unconfessed can hinder the exercise of the priestly office by the least of all believers. "By Jesus Christ" he has been made "acceptable to God," and only personal pollution can now hinder the realization of those precious privileges in the presence of God.

All evangelism must begin with prayer. And no human service, or device, can take the place of the intercession of a priest who is cleansed, and "acceptable to God," even in the holiest place "by Jesus Christ."

While the believer-priest may intercede in behalf of his fellow-members in the body of Christ, it is a privilege of his co-partnership with Christ to intercede for the lost; and the answer to that prayer will be the going forth of the Spirit to convince them of sin, of righteousness, and of judgment.

The importance of preaching and teaching the truth is in no way lessened by this emphasis upon priestly prayer. It must only be borne in mind that prevailing prayer necessarily accompanies all other ministry; for it commands the power of God, and secures the needed illumination of the mind toward the Word that may be preached. Without prayer there will be little understanding and vision of the Gospel, even though faithfully presented.

The reason for human intercession in the divine plan has not been wholly revealed. The repeated statements of Scripture that it is a necessary link in the chain that carries the divine energy into the impotent souls of men, in addition to its actual achievement as seen in the world, must be the sufficient evidence of the imperative need for the prayer in connection with the purpose of God. Thus in the Scriptures and in experience it is revealed that God has honored man with an exalted place of co-operation and partnership with Himself in His great projects of human transformation.

Among the many direct and positive promises wherein the activity of the divine power is conditioned on human faithfulness in prayer but one will here be quoted and considered.

In John 14:14, it is written: "If ye shall ask anything in my name, I will do it" (see also John 15:16, 23, 24, and Luke 11:9). In this Scripture the assignment of both the divine and the human part in the work is clearly seen; for the bald outline of this passage is, "If ye shall ask, . . . I will do." Thus God reserves to Himself the undertaking and accomplishment of every object of human intercession, and assigns to man the service of prayer. This is quite reasonable; for it is evident that the accomplishment of any spiritual transformation must ever be His to do, since its consummation is possible to divine strength alone. Thus, though man cannot do the important task, he is permitted, through intercession, to cooperate with God in its accomplishment, and to fulfill, according to revelation, a necessary part in the divine program.

Prayer is said to be a cause. It is because of prayer that God promises to do. He is pleased to work through preaching; but his mighty undertakings are conditioned on prayer. Effective preaching is one of the necessary means in answering faithful prayer. It is said in Rom. 10:13, 14, that the unsaved cannot hear without a preacher; yet it is equally true that the preaching, to be effective, must be in the "demonstration and power of the Holy Spirit."

It should be noted that, under these conditions and relationships, stated in John 14:14, every true prayer is not only an acknowledgment of God as the only sufficient One, but it demands an attitude of entire expectation from Him on the part of the supplicant. This is essential if normal relations are to exist between God and man. The answer to prayer, when the expectation is not wholly toward God, would but divert the confidence of man, and foster a false trust in his mind. It is necessary for man, therefore, in the interests of his own understanding of God and truth, to come directly to God, acknowledging His omnipotence, and looking to Him as alone sufficient to do the thing for which he may be praying.

Again, it may be seen from this promise that God, to some extent, has seen fit to condition His action upon the believer's prayer; for the Scripture says: "If ye shall ask anything in my name, I will do it"; and this is the secret of all true evangelism.

There is another promise bearing directly on this point: "If any man see his brother sin a sin which is not unto death, he shall ask, and he shall give him life for them that sin not unto death. There is a sin unto death: I do not say that he shall pray for it" (1 John 5:16).

It is, then, the teaching of Scripture that the action of the mighty power of God in convicting and illuminating the unsaved is also, in a large measure, dependent upon the priestly intercession of the believer. This, too, is a conspicuous fact in experience as revealed in history. Where believing prayer has been offered with expectation toward God alone, there has always been evidence of the power of God unto salvation, according to His covenant promises. These periods of refreshing have been called "revivals." The immediate blessing resulting from the adjustment of believers to the program of God is natural; but the certain return to an attitude of indifference, on the human side, has made that brief season of blessing seem to be some special visitation from heaven when God was thought to have been "on the giving hand." It may have been impossible in such a case, for the extra meetings and methods to have continued; but the blessing was in no way conditioned on the meetings or methods. Intercessory prayer, the real basis of the blessing, could and should have continued. The marvelous, and so little experienced, movings of the Spirit upon the unsaved are at the command of the least of God's children, if that one be cleansed; for such a believer is a priest unto God, and no limitation of times and seasons is set in the New Testament upon his intercession.

How little the stupendous fact of this individual power in prayer is realized by Christians today! The present failure on the part of Christians to enter the holy place in intercession according to the appointment of God is sufficient to account for the present lack of Holy Spirit conviction and conversion in the church.

The neglect and ignorance of the facts regarding the believer's privileges in prayer, when those facts are so clearly stated in the Scriptures, can be explained only in the light of the revealed Satanic opposition to the purpose of God; for intercessory prayer is a strategic point for the attack of this arch enemy inasmuch as the mighty movements of the Spirit for salvation are, for the present time, awaiting this human co-operation.

If there are exceptions in the history of ingatherings where there have been what seemed to be unprayed-for outpourings of the Spirit, in no case can it be proven that prayer was not offered. In every case where the Spirit seemed to descend upon the church with sovereign power, there has been either an appalling spiritual death in the church, or a new emphasis has been needed upon some neglected truth in evangelism. Such seasons have been so rare in the history of the church that they can be counted only as exceptions, and should in no way be used to qualify the revealed plan of God, which He has blessed throughout the years.

Not only are the priceless results of the saving power of God hindered, but the individual believer has suffered unmeasured loss in his possible reward, when the prayer of intercession has for any reason ceased. Prayer presents the greatest opportunity for soul-winning, and there is precious reward promised to those who bring souls to Christ, and are found to be suffering with Him in His burden for the lost.

Fundamentally, then, the personal element in true soul-winning work is more a service of pleading *for* souls than a service of pleading *with* souls. It is talking with God about men from a clean heart and in the power of the Spirit, rather than talking to men about God. But let no one conclude that such intercessory prayer is not a service demanding time and vitality. If faithfully entered into this ministry, as has been pointed out, will result in an opportunity to direct Spirit-moved men to the faithful provisions and promises of God.

Chapter 5

Suffering with Christ

It should not be concluded from what has gone before that there is no other God-appointed human service in behalf of the lost than the prayer of intercession. It is true, however, that intercessory prayer is the first and most important service. As has been stated, the divine order is to talk to God about men, until the door is definitely open to talk to men about God. Any service which He may appoint after believing prayer has been offered will be wonderfully blessed by Him. But to intrude upon strangers, unless positively led to do so, or to implore unwilling and unprepared men, is to display a zeal without knowledge, and is fraught with peril to immortal souls. Such boldness is often urged and commended as being a high form of Christian service; yet no Spirit-filled person can rush ahead of the movements of God without a deep sense of protest from the Spirit Who indwells him. It is not altogether due to personal diffidence that true believers often find it difficult to speak to the unsaved about their need of Christ. There may be a restraint upon such service; for if the unsaved are not prepared by the Spirit, any attempt to force a decision may be a violation of the plan of God.

If space could be given here to incidents illustrating the necessity of waiting *on* God and *for* God as the first effort to be made for the salvation of any person, it would be apparent that the preparation of one soul may require many years, or this preparation may be accomplished in another in as many hours;

but seldom is it advantageous to press the decision until some evidence is given that the Spirit is leading toward such an appeal. Such quiet waiting will always be rewarded; for, as in the days as recorded in the Acts of the Apostles, there will usually be some clear indication from the illuminated person that the heart is prepared, although it be but a look or action, which will be a sufficient assurance that the way is open for any necessary word to be spoken which will direct that heart to its acceptance of Christ. Coaxing and pleading will be found to be unnecessary, for the soul will be thirsting for the Water of Life. When led of the Spirit, the child of God must be as ready to wait as to go, as prepared to be silent as to speak.

The precious service of leading the enlightened person to a decision is often appointed to the one who has first suffered for that person in intercession. This is the real place of so-called "personal work," and too much cannot be said as to the value of the careful preparation and instruction of every believer for this particular service; for there is need of great clearness and skill in explaining the exact terms of the Gospel to the one upon whom the Spirit is moving in conviction and illumination. The whole plan of salvation should be clearly understood, and those texts and passages kept in mind which are adapted to meet the mental confusion that Satan produces in those with whom the Spirit is dealing.

There is need also of a clear understanding of the great distinctions between the saved and the unsaved, and God's entire plan of dealing with each. A child of God who has long been "walking in darkness" will often appear as an unregenerate soul; yet the Spirit will not deal with him as such, and his way back into fellowship with God must be by confession alone, and not by an unscriptural second conversion.

Above all, the personal worker must be wholly dependent upon the leading of the Spirit. He should be as prepared to do the unusual thing as the usual. If really prepared for service, his ear will be open to God concerning every person he may chance to meet, but he will not assume to force a decision without divine direction. With the great commission to preach the gospel to every creature, it may usually be assumed that God would have us speak to men, with all earnestness, unless otherwise led by the Spirit. There is an important distinction to be considered between presenting the Gospel of saving grace to a company of men, and demanding an immediate decision from an individual. A personal decision should be pressed only when so led by the Spirit.

All true service for God is the ministry of the Spirit through the believer (Rom. 12:3-8; 1 Cor. 12:4-31), and it is therefore vain to form hard and fast rules by which we intend to do this service. God will direct a yielded life in service which He has appointed in His sovereign power and grace. Compassion for lost souls will be created in the heart by the Spirit, and this will find expression and relief in the Spirit-inspired prayer of intercession. The Spirit will then answer this prayer by going forth through some ministry of the Word, with convicting and converting power to the glory of Christ.

The Highest Form of Human Suffering

The burden of heart that can find no peace because of the lost condition of some individual is the highest form of human suffering, and is several times referred to in the Scriptures. There this burden for the lost is seen, not only to form a part of human suffering, but to be a normal experience in the life of every saved person. That it is not a common experience among Christians today can be explained only by the fact that there are abnormal conditions in many Christian lives.

The reality of human suffering and its place in a Christian's life is so vital a part of true evangelism, and occupies so conspicuous a place in the New Testament, that it should be considered sufficiently at length to distinguish that particular part of suffering which has to do with the salvation of the lost from its other aspects.

The believer may suffer *for* Christ. This form of suffering may include the involuntary sacrifice of the loss of friends, property, reputation, or health, and the voluntary sacrifice or separation from loved ones, gifts, humiliation and faithful service, even unto death. It is stated in Phil. 1:29 that such suffering is a gift to the believer: "Unto you it is given in behalf of Christ, not only to believe on him, but also to suffer for his sake." Unto you it is given to be parted from loved ones in the world-wide ministry of the Gospel, to become poor that others may become rich, to suffer separation or privation as a sacrifice for Him.

This form of suffering was experienced by the Lord of Glory, and to those who are in the midst of these afflictions it is said: "The sufferings of this present time are not worthy to be compared with the glory that shall be revealed in us"; and "Our light affliction, which is but for a moment, worketh for us a far more exceeding and eternal weight of glory."

Suffering 'with' Christ

The suffering of a Christian according to the Scriptures is primarily suffering with Christ. This is attested by various passages (1 Pet. 4:13; Rom. 8:17; Col. 1:24; Phil. 2:5-9; and 2 Tim. 2:12). The important word used in connection with the believer's relation to Christian suffering is "with" and that word emphasizes the necessary distinction that much of the suffering in the world is alien to fellowship with Christ. On the other hand, this word suggests a vital union and divine co-partnership between the suffering believer and his suffering Lord.

In suffering with Christ the Christian may either suffer from man the reproaches of Christ, or he may come to experience with Christ a divinely wrought burden and sorrow for the lost. Beyond this it is impossible for any believer to go in the mystery of the sufferings of Christ; for what He suffered from God in becoming Himself an offering for sin could not be shared by any other, though one might greatly desire a similar ministry. (See Rom. 9:1-3.)

Suffering *with* Christ is a natural phase of a Christian's life and experience. He is sojourning in an enemy's land, is called to be a witness against its sin, and is summoned to labor that souls may be saved from its evil and darkness. "If the world hate you, ye know that it hated me before it hated you. If ye were of the world, the world would love his own; but because ye are not of the world, but I have chosen you out of the world, therefore the world hateth you" (John 15:18, 19). To those who did not believe on Him He said: "The world cannot hate you; but me it hateth, because I testify of it, that the works thereof are evil" (John 7:7). "It is enough for the disciple that he be as his master, and the servant as his lord. If they have called the master of the house Beelzebub, how much more shall they call them of his household?" (Matt. 10:25). "As thou has sent me into the world, even so have I also sent them into the world" (John 17:18). "Beloved, think it not strange concerning the fiery trial which is to try you, as though some strange thing happened unto you: but rejoice, inasmuch as ye are partakers of Christ's sufferings: that when his glory shall be revealed, ye may be glad also with exceeding joy" (1 Pet. 4:12, 13).

So also, as is seen by these passages, suffering with Christ here is the only possible path into the reward of being glorified together with Him over there. This is not salvation, for salvation cannot be gained by any degree of human suffering. It is rather that for which the glorious crown and reward is to be given to the faithful in their co-partnership with Christ. This truth is emphasized in the following passage: "Let this mind be in you, which was also in Christ Jesus: Who, being in the form of God, thought it not robbery to be equal with God: but made himself of no reputation, and took upon him the form of a servant, and was made in the likeness of men: and being found in fashion as a man, he humbled himself and became obedient unto death, even the death of the cross. Wherefore God also hath highly exalted him, and given him a name which is above every name: that at the name of Jesus every knee should bow, of things in heaven, and things in earth, and things under the earth; and that every tongue should confess that Jesus Christ is Lord, to the glory of God the Father" (Phil. 2:5-11).

Here it is inferred that the believer is to allow the mind of Christ to be reproduced in him by the power of God (Phil. 2:13), and these seven successive steps in the path of Christ, from His native place in the glory to the felon's death on the cross, are reviewed in this Scripture in order that such steps may be admitted in the Christian's life, who is to be "as his Lord" even in this world. It is also inferred in this passage that, through this relation to Jesus in suffering, there is to be an identity with Him in His glory. "The Spirit itself beareth witness with our spirit, that we are the children of God: and if children, then heirs; heirs of God, and joint-heirs with Christ; if so be that we suffer with him, that we may be also glorified together. For I reckon that the sufferings of this present time are not worthy to be compared with the glory which shall be revealed in us" (Rom. 8:16-18). "It is a faithful saying: For if we be dead with him, we shall also live with him: if we suffer, we shall also reign with him: if we deny him he also will deny us" (2 Tim. 2:11, 12).

Paul's Ministry of Suffering

Suffering was the ministry to which Paul was appointed by the Lord through the disciple Ananias when the Lord commanded Ananias: "Go thy way: for he is a chosen vessel unto me, to bear my name before the Gentiles, and kings, and the children of Israel: for I will show him how great things he must suffer for my name's sake" (Acts 9:15, 16).

Thus it may be concluded that, while all the mystery of suffering is not explained, and probably cannot be, it is an essential part of the Christian's life and union with Christ in this world, and of identification with Him in His glory.

Of that suffering which is from man and because of the believer's relation and loyalty to Christ it is said: "Beloved, think it not strange concerning the fiery trial which is to try you, as though some strange thing happened unto you: but rejoice, inasmuch as ye are partakers of Christ's sufferings; that when his glory shall be revealed, ye may be glad also with exceeding joy. If ye be reproached for the name of Christ, happy are ye; for the spirit of glory and of God resteth upon you: on their part he is evil spoken of, but on your part he is glorified. But let none of you suffer as a murderer, or as a thief, or as an evil doer, or as a busybody in other men's matters. Yet if any man suffer as a Christian, let him not be ashamed; but let him glorify God on this behalf" (1 Pet. 4:12-16).

It is, however, sympathetic suffering that enters most directly into the movements of the power of God in evangelism. As a mother's face may reflect more pain than the face of her suffering child, so there is an unlimited realm of possible suffering in sympathy and burden for another. This highest and deepest suffering is born of two parents, which are love and appreciation. The brute may love its offspring, but cannot appreciate its sufferings; while a savage may appreciate pain, but cares little for the suffering one. To the one who both knows and feels there is revealed a degree of the mystery of suffering in sympathy.

When the sufferings of Christ are contemplated in the light of this simple fact, it will be seen that lack of the death of Christ is, on the part of God, first of all the infinite wisdom, vision and power to appreciate. He comprehended man's sin, his eternal ruin, and necessary banishment from His presence. And second, He loved the world of men enough to act mightily in their behalf. That He loved them is the reason of His effort for them. That He appreciated their terrible need was the warrant for the particular thing He did. The measure of His appreciation and love is unbounded; for "He bore our sins in his own body on the tree," which reveals the reality of our sins as viewed by an infinite God. He became the propitiation for the sins of the whole world.

It was not the love of God alone that was revealed in the death of Christ. His eternal wisdom and Godhead are seen as well by the particular thing which He did for man's redemption. In that death He also disclosed His estimate of man's need. So the cross is, in the mind and heart of the Infinite, both a warning of doom and a wooing of love; and it is no credit to finite man that he denies the voice of the Infinite, rejects His verdict of human hopelessness, and misinterprets the value and vision of the death of Christ.

The dominant motive that prompted the sufferings of Christ was revealed in one of His prayers at the cross. Had His suffering been physical alone, His prayer might have been, Father, they are causing Me physical pain; or had His sufferings been His personal sacrifice alone, He might have prayed, Father, they are taking My life from Me. In reality He prayed, "Father, forgive them, for they know not what they do." And while the sufferings of His body and the sacrifice of His life constituted an offering for sin, "once for all," these were prompted by the divine vision of human need and His yearning compassion for lost and ruined men; for he prayed not for himself but for them. In that mysterious suffering for the sin of the world no human can suffer with Christ. That suffering was final and complete. It can only be believed in and appropriated by the one who has come to realize his own share in it.

When a soul has received the redemption which is in Christ and is saved, that one is then privileged to suffer with Christ in a compassion for the lost—being prompted, in some measure, by the same divine vision and love, through the presence and power of the indwelling Spirit.

This is illustrated by the testimony of the Apostle Paul in Rom. 9:1-8: "I say the truth in Christ, I lie not, my conscience also bearing me witness in the Holy Ghost, that I have great heaviness and continual sorrow in my heart. For I could wish that I myself were accursed from Christ for my brethren, my kinsmen according to the flesh."

Much is said in the preceding context of the power and blessing of the Spirit indwelling the Christian. In this passage, however, he is seen lifting the Apostle Paul to a similar viewpoint as that which Christ occupied, when He was willing to be accursed that lost men might be saved, and which he experienced when He cried, "My God, my God, why hast thou forsaken me?" From this point of divine vision Paul longs, too, with an unutterable longing to make some sufficient sacrifice, even an impossible and terrible separation from Christ his Lord, if only his brethren, his kinsmen after the flesh, might be saved. This attitude of agonizing suffering for the salvation of his brethren was not an element of the human nature of Saul, who found his delight in the condemnation and execution of his brethren when they were found to be followers of Jesus; nor is this divine touch found in any unregenerate life. It is the love of God shed abroad in our hearts by the Holy Spirit which is given unto us, or in reality, the very love of God reaching out for the lost through the believer. (See also John 15:12, 13; Gal. 5:22.) This experience of Paul's is possible to others. By the Indwelling One, the believer may come both to appreciate the lost estate of men and to experience a divine compassion for them.

The Deepest Meaning of Suffering

Suffering with Christ, then, in its deepest meaning, is to come to experience by the Spirit an unutterable agony for men out of

Christ, and from that vision and love to be willing to offer personal sacrifice or endure physical pain, if need be, that they may be saved. This is as near to "a cross" as the Christian can come in experience; for he can make no atonement, nor is human atonement needed. As his eyes are opened and his heart is made sensitive to the indescribable need of any soul out of Christ, he has, to that extent, experienced the divine compassion "shed abroad in his heart." Such suffering with Christ is the heritage of every regenerate soul.

One has but to recall the spiritual agony of soul, like the physical pain of a woman in travail, that has borne down upon believers in connection with the birth of souls in the great in-gatherings of history to understand the reality of divinely wrought suffering with Christ, which is granted to the believer, and is the sure warrant of identification with Him in His glory. So, whenever a believer is prepared to receive this great gift of suffering with Christ, it will be granted unto him to such a degree, and at such times as he is able to bear it. All pity for those Christians who, through want of adjustment to the mind and purpose of God, are never so privileged!

When the heavenly riches and rewards, with the eternal blessedness of one soul that is saved are considered, how great is the price we pay for our indifference toward the unsaved about us on every hand! Could we but get one glimpse of this life with its priceless opportunities, as it will be seen in retrospect from the glory, we would suffer nothing to divert us from that unbroken walk with God in which He would impart all His own passion and love to our hearts and cause us to be instant in season and out of season in the winning of souls.

There is a great lost world of individuals surrounding every believer, and if his heart is attuned to the Spirit Who indwells him, he cannot but suffer at times with Christ in an agony of soul that they may be saved. That soul-anguish in a believer may find its expression only in "groanings which cannot be uttered." In this extremity, he will be driven into the holiest place, and he will find no relief except in the priestly prayer of intercession.

Through such intercession the Spirit is covenanted to go forward to deal with unregenerate men, and by His mighty Sword to strike the blindness from their eyes, and to bring them face to face with the salvation that is in Jesus Christ.

It will be observed that this divine burden for the lost is a very uncommon experience among believers today; and the solution of this problem is found in the last step that marks the movements of the "power of God unto salvation." The difficulty lies in the defilement of the believers who are priests before God and who do not and cannot, because of their own unfitness, experience the love of God for others, or prevail with God in the holy place.

Chapter 6

The Cleansing of the Priests

The various conditions on which the answer to prayer depends, as set forth in the New Testament, require an experience in the supplicant of common vision and sympathy with the mind and will of God. "If ye abide in me and my words abide in you," is a condition which demands a relation to God on the part of the individual, wherein both the present leading of God is realized and His written will is known. To abide in Christ is to keep His commandments (John 15:10), and to be in close fellowship with Him. To have His Word abiding in us is to be instructed in the Scriptures; and to one who has thus been brought into full sympathy with the purpose of God, it can safely be said, "Ye shall ask what ye will, and it shall be done unto you." This promise of prayer, then, is not unlimited, as is sometimes supposed, but is qualified by a required adjustment to the will of God of the mind and heart of the one who prays. So, also, the oft-repeated condition, "In my name" admits of only such themes in prayer as can reasonably be coupled with the glory of Christ and the projects of His unfinished work in the world.

Another condition of prayer is given in Mark 11:24: "Therefore I say unto you, What things soever ye desire, when ye pray, believe that ye receive them, and ye shall have them." This condition does not include every subject of prayer; for it would be impossible to believe that God would grant anything inconsistent with His own purpose or Being. Yet with all this nearness to the mind of God there will be many legitimate objects of prayer, concerning the wisdom of which the believer must ever be in doubt; for all requests in prayer naturally fall into two classes at the point of the known will of God. When there is no revelation, the supplicator can never pass the boundary of the qualifying words, "Thy will, not mine, be done." But when there is a revelation of the will of God, this boundary is done away: and to be uncertain of the will of God, when His will is clearly revealed, is but to doubt the Word through which He has made it manifest.

The priestly intercession of the believer, which is a necessary element in true evangelism, falls in the realm of this latter phase of prayer. This prayer is nothing less than the mighty movings of the "power of God unto salvation," since the Spirit indites the intercession. It is a glorious human co-partnership with the divine Shepherd in His solicitude and effort to seek the lost.

Every possible question as to the divine will in the salvation, sanctification and glorification of men has been wholly answered in the revelation of the heart of God through the sacrifice on the cross. His eternal power and Godhead were revealed in the things created; "For the invisible things of him from the creation of the world are clearly seen, being understood by the things that are made, even his eternal power and Godhead" (Rom. 1:20). His soul-saving compassion and desire for helpless men were revealed in the cross of Christ; as it is written: "No man hath seen God at any time; the only begotten Son, which is in the bosom of the Father, he hath declared him" (John 1:18). "For God so loved the world, that he gave his only begotten Son, that whosoever believeth in him should not perish, but have everlasting life" (John 3:16). "For this is good and acceptable in the sight of God our Savior; who will have all men to be saved, and to come unto the knowledge of the truth" (1 Tim. 2:3, 4). "God was in Christ, reconciling the world unto himself" (2 Cor. 5:19).

From the foregoing Scriptures it will be found that there has been a completion of all the grounds of salvation, and a sufficient revelation of the purpose and will of God for the redemption of all men through the cross of Christ; and since His covenant-promises, relating to prayer, are still in force, it is clear that all hindrances to the movements of God in salvation must be due to some failure on the human side. Either the believers do not meet their high privilege in the holy place, or the unsaved, when convicted, reject the vision that is given unto them. Since there is little evidence of any new vision received, or rejected, on the part of the unregenerate, the solution of the question as to why there is not more saving power among believers today must be sought for in the realm of the believer's ministry of intercession.

It has already been pointed out that, while there may be little demand for purification in the exercise of gifts, where the service is only between man and man, there can be no entering into the holy place without the laving or removal of defilement, which God alone may see. This cleansing has been typified by the laver that stood at the entrance to the "Holy of holies" in the tabernacle of old. The necessity for that special cleansing of the priest before he approached the presence of Jehovah "in the tent of meeting" was emphasized by the penalty of death if the cleansing was neglected. The passage in Ex. 30:17-21 is here given:

"And the Lord spoke unto Moses, saying, Thou shalt also make a laver of brass, and his foot also of brass, to wash withal: and thou shalt put it between the tabernacle of the congregation and the altar, and thou shalt put water therein. For Aaron and his sons shall wash their hands and their feet thereat: when they go into the tabernacle of the congregation, they shall wash with water, that they die not; or when they come near to the altar to minister, to burn offering made by fire unto the Lord: so they shall wash their hands and their feet, that they die not: and it shall be a statute for ever to them, even to him and his seed throughout their generations."

The restatement of this truth is found in several passages in the New Testament in which the cleansing and refitting of the believer-priest is set forth. In John 13:3-11, Jesus speaks of the first tense of salvation as the whole bath ("he that is bathed") ; and, in contrast to this, He also speaks of His own work in removing the believer's defilement which may have been received through contact with the world. This cleansing of the believer is typified by the bathing of the feet. This is most suggestive, when compared with the one preparatory whole bath of the Aaronic priest, which was required when he entered the priestly office (Ex. 29:4), and the necessary repeated laving before each entrance into the holy place in the course of his priestly ministry.

John 13:3-11, which teaches the possible cleansing of the believer-priest, is as follows: "Jesus knowing that the Father had given all things into his hands, and that he was come from God, and went to God; he riseth from supper, and laid aside his garments; and took a towel, and girded himself. After that he poureth water into a bason, and began to wash the disciples' feet, and to wipe them with the towel wherewith he was girded. Then cometh he to Simon Peter: and Peter saith unto him, Lord, dost Thou wash my feet? Jesus answered and said unto him, What I do Thou knowest not now; but thou shalt know hereafter. Peter saith unto him, Thou shalt never wash my feet. Jesus answered him, If I wash thee not, thou hast no part with me. Simon Peter saith unto him, Lord, not my feet only, but also my hands and my head. Jesus saith to him, he that is washed needeth not save to wash his feet, but is clean every whit: and ye are clean, but not all. For he knew who should betray him; therefore said he, Ye are not all clean."

On this passage, Dr. C. I. Scofield gives the following note in the *Scofield Reference Bible*: "The underlying imagery is of an oriental returning from the public bath to his home. His feet would contract defilement and require cleansing, but not his body. So the believer is cleansed as before the law from all sin once for all (Heb. 10:1-12), but needs ever to bring his daily sins to the Father in confession, that he may abide in unbroken fellowship with the Father and with the Son (1 John 1:1-10). The blood of Christ answers forever to all the law could say as to the believer's guilt, but he needs constant cleansing from the defilement of sin. (See Eph. 5:25-27; 1 John 5:6.) Typically, the order of approach to the presence of God was, first, the brazen altar of sacrifice, and then the laver of cleansing (Ex. 40:6, 7). See, also, the order in Ex. 30:17-21: Christ cannot have communion with a defiled saint, but He can and will cleanse him."

Other passages on the cleansing of the New Testament priest should be quoted also: "Husbands, love your wives, even as

Christ also loved the church, and gave himself for it; that he might sanctify and cleanse it with the washing of water by the word, that he might present it to himself a glorious church, not having spot, or wrinkle, or any such thing; but that it should be holy and without blemish" (Eph. 5:23-27). "If we say that we have fellowship with him, and walk in darkness, we lie, and do not the truth: but if we walk in the light, as he is in the light, we have fellowship one with another, and the blood of Jesus Christ his Son cleanseth us from all sin. If we say that we have no sin, we deceive ourselves, and the truth is not in us. If we confess our sins, he is faithful and just to forgive us our sins, and to cleanse us from all unrighteousness" (1 John 1:6-9). "Nevertheless the foundation of God standeth sure, having this seal, the Lord knoweth them that are his. And, let every one that nameth the name of Christ depart from iniquity. But in a great house there are not only vessels of gold and of silver, but also of wood and of earth; and some to honor and some to dishonor. If a man therefore purge himself from these, he shall be a vessel unto honor, sanctified, and meet for the master's use, and prepared unto every good work" (2 Tim. 2:19-21).

The Aaronic priest met the penalty of instant death if he attempted to enter the Holy of holies without the laving that was prescribed by the law, and while that penalty is not continued under grace it is evident that there is no prevailing power in prayer or effectiveness in ministry so long as the believer's sin and defilement are not put away. As the priest of the Old Testament failed in his office through unfitness before God, so the priest of the New Testament, from the same cause, may lose much of his privilege in holy service and communion with Christ. His priestly ministry of sacrifice, in which he presents his body, his praise and his benevolence, may go on in their outward forms, he being under grace; yet it cannot be effectual when, because of sin, it is a ministry that is not acceptable to God. So also his priestly ministry of intercession may become of no avail through defilement.

Here, as in the ministry of sacrifice, the loss is immeasurable. Not only are all his possible services to God and blessings to men hindered, which might be realized through his ministry in the holiest place, but he is without the joy and peace of fellowship with Christ. It is of great importance for the believer to realize that through his defilement, not only his priestly ministry is hindered, but his own fellowship with Christ is lost as well. "If we say that we have fellowship with him, and walk in darkness, we lie, and do not the truth: but if we walk in the light, as he is in the light, we have fellowship one with another, and the blood of Jesus Christ his Son cleanseth us from all sin" (1 John 1:6, 7). "These things [about abiding in Christ] have I spoken unto you, that my joy might remain in you, and that your joy might be full" (John 15:11). "Verily, verily, I say unto you, Whatsoever ye shall ask the Father in my name, he will give it you. Hitherto ye have asked nothing in my name: ask, and ye shall receive, that your joy may be full" (John 16:23, 24). "And now I come to thee; and these things I speak in the world, that they might have my joy fulfilled in themselves" (John 17:13). "That which we have seen and heard declare we unto you, that ye also may have fellowship with us: and truly our fellowship is with the Father, and with his Son Jesus Christ. And these things write we unto you, that your joy may be full" (1 John 1:3, 4).

It may be concluded from the foregoing testimony that defilement in the believer hinders every phase of his priestly office, makes fellowship with Christ impossible, and robs him of his personal joy and blessing.

The limitation that is placed upon the priestly prayer of intercession through undealt-with sin in the believer's life is the only aspect of this truth which is directly related to the subject of evangelism.

The following Scriptures warrant the conclusion that sin directly hinders prevailing prayer:

"If I regard iniquity in my heart, the Lord will not hear me" (Psa. 66:18). "Behold, the Lord's hand is not shortened, that it cannot save; neither his ear heavy that it cannot hear: but your iniquities have separated between you and your God, and your sins have hid his face from you, that he will not hear" (Isa. 59:1, 2). "Therefore if thou bring thy gift to the altar, and there rememberest that thy brother hath ought against thee; leave there thy gift before the altar, and go thy way: first be reconciled to thy brother, and then come and offer thy gift" (Matt.

5:23, 24). "If ye abide in me, and my words abide in you, ye shall ask what ye will, and it shall be done unto you" (John 15:7). "I will therefore that men pray everywhere, lifting up holy hands, without wrath and doubting" (1 Tim. 2:8). "Ye lust, and have not: ye kill, and desire to have, and cannot obtain: ye fight and war, yet ye have not, because ye ask not. Ye ask, and receive not, because ye ask amiss, that ye may consume it upon your lusts" (James 4:2, 3). "Confess your faults one to another, and pray one for another, that ye may be healed. The effectual fervent prayer of a righteous man availeth much" (James 5:16). "Likewise, ye husbands, dwell with them according to knowledge, giving honor unto the wife, as unto the weaker vessel, and as being heirs together of the grace of life; that your prayers be not hindered" (1 Pet. 3:7).

There is no point more strategic for the subtle attack of Satan against the plan and work of God in saving men than the point where God offers to meet the Christian for cleansing; for, if cleansing can be hindered, very much of human cooperation with God in "seeking the lost" is hindered also. This Satanic influence is seen first in the fact that Christians are almost universally ignorant of the God-provided way by which they may be cleansed from their defilement; and second, this Satanic influence is seen in the tendency of the flesh to resist the necessary requirements of God, even when they are understood.

The definite offer to the unregenerate person of the forgiveness of his sins is conditioned upon his receiving Christ as his personal Savior, and there is equally as definite an offer to the Christian for the forgiveness of his sin and defilement. The condition which is imposed upon the believer is that he confess his sins. "If we confess our sins, he is faithful and just to forgive us our sins, and to cleanse us from all unrighteousness" (1 John 2:9). This passage never applies to the unsaved.

The offer of forgiveness to the unsaved and the offer of forgiveness to the saved should never be confused. While both are made possible by the blood of Christ, the sin question with the unsaved is dealt with as a part of the whole first tense of salvation, which cannot be divided, and is likened by Christ to the whole bath: while the sin question with the saved person stands alone, since no other aspect of his glorious salvation is disturbed by his sin. Hence the removal of his defilement is all that is called for, and is likened by Christ to the bathing of the feet of one who is returning from the whole bath. The "Prodigal Son" presents an illustration of the way in which a Christian may return to fellowship and blessing. There is no record that he was any less a son "in the far country" than he was in his own home; nor is it recorded of him that he returned to his father's house on the basis of sacrifice or atonement; but it is stated that he returned on the basis of confession; for it is said that he arose and came to his father, and said unto him, "Father, I have sinned against heaven, and in thy sight, and am no more worthy to be called thy son."

In this same connection it may be seen that confession is the only requirement which can reasonably be demanded of a sinning saint; for the basis of any true fellowship is a symphonizing of thought and purpose. Hence any defilement in a believer, of necessity, interrupts his fellowship though not his salvation with a holy God. When fellowship with God is broken by sin, it can be re-established only by a frank admission of guilt and failure on the part of the sinning one. To refuse a confession is to contend that right is wrong, and wrong is right, which would be a contradiction of the very nature and character of God.

Confession re-opens the way for fellowship with God and of access to God, but it does not in any way atone for sin. Propitiation for sin was perfectly accomplished at the cross. Since His ascension, Christ has been continually pleading the efficacy of His own sacrificial death for sin in behalf of believers (Rom. 8:33, 34; Heb. 7:25). Therefore, it is said to the Christian: "If we confess our sins, he is faithful and just to forgive us our sins, and to cleanse us from all unrighteousness." The sin of the saved one is not forgiven on the grounds of an immediate act of mercy, but is forgiven on the grounds of the sacrifice made "once for all" at the cross. So it is said that God is faithful and just to forgive us our sins, rather than that He is tender and merciful to forgive us our sins.

The importance of confession of sin and of self-judgment is mentioned also in 1 Cor. 11:31, 32. "For if we would judge ourselves, we should not be judged. But when we are judged, we are chastened of the Lord, that we should not be condemned with the world." In considering this important passage, it may be noted:

I. This Scripture, like that relating to confession of sin, is addressed only to believers.

II. The believer is first given the opportunity to judge himself before God, and if he fails in voluntary self-judgment, God will judge him by chastisement.

III. And the chastisement of God is given that His child may not be condemned with the world. In this connection it should be remembered that God is in covenant with His children to the effect that they "shall not be brought into condemnation." "Verily, verily, I say unto you, He that heareth my word, and believeth on him that sent me, hath everlasting life, and shall not come into condemnation; but is passed from death unto life" (John 5:24). So again, "There is therefore now no condemnation to them which are in Christ Jesus" (Rom. 8:1).

The whole relation between the believer and his God is one of eternal sonship, which cannot be broken; hence all the judgments of God upon His own are for correction, while His judgments of the unsaved are unto condemnation. "He that believeth on him is not condemned; but he that believeth not is condemned already, because he hath not believed in the name of the only begotten Son of God" (John 3:18).

The same family relationship of father to the son is carried through both the Old and the New Testaments. "I will be his father, and he shall be my son. If he commit iniquity, I will chasten him with the rod of men, and with the stripes of the children of men: but my mercy shall not depart away from him, as I took it from Saul, whom I put away before thee" (2 Sam. 7:14, 15). "And David said unto Nathan, I have sinned against the Lord. And Nathan said unto David, The Lord also has put away thy sin; thou shalt not die. Howbeit, because by this deed thou hast given great occasion to the enemies of the Lord to blaspheme, the child also that is born unto thee shall surely die" (2 Sam. 12:13, 14). "To deliver such an one unto Satan for the destruction of the flesh, that the spirit may be saved in the day of the Lord Jesus" (1 Cor. 5:5).

"For consider him that endured such contradiction of sinners against himself, lest ye be wearied and faint in your minds. Ye have not yet resisted unto blood, striving against sin. And ye have forgotten the exhortation, which speaketh unto you as unto children, My son, despise not thou the chastening of the Lord, nor faint when thou art rebuked of him: for whom the Lord loveth he chasteneth, and scourgeth every son whom he receiveth. If ye endure chastening, God dealeth with you as with sons; for what son is he whom the father chasteneth not? But if ye be without chastisement, whereof all are partakers, then are ye bastards, and not sons. Furthermore we have had fathers of our flesh which corrected us, and we gave them reverence: shall we not much rather be in subjection unto the Father of spirits, and live? For they verily for a few days chastened us after their own pleasure; but he for our profit, that we might be partakers of his holiness. Now no chastening for the present seemeth to be joyous, but grievous: nevertheless afterwards it yieldeth the peaceable fruit of righteousness unto them which are exercised thereby. Wherefore lift up the hands which hang down, and the feeble knees; and make straight paths for your feet, lest that which is lame be turned out of the way; but let it rather be healed. Follow peace with all men, and holiness, without which no man shall see the Lord: looking diligently lest any man fail of the grace of God; lest any root of bitterness springing up trouble you, and thereby many be defiled" (Heb. 12:3-15). "Every branch in me that beareth not fruit he taketh it away: and every branch that beareth fruit, he purgeth it, that it may bring forth more fruit" (John 15:2).

From this extensive body of Scripture it will be found that the Christian is privileged to "walk in the light, as he is in the light," which does not necessarily mean a sinless life: but it does mean the humble confession of all the fruits of a sinful nature, and an attitude of willingness to meet every demand of God for the putting away of sin. If the confession of sin and the judgment of self is not willingly entered into, there must be a chastisement from God, lest the believer be condemned with the world. The execution of this chastisement, it would seem, is sometimes committed to Satan (1 Cor. 5:5; 1 Tim. 1:20). If fruit is not borne after chastisement, then God taketh the branch away (John 15:2). This is not a loss of salvation, but is an entire removal from earthly life and service.

There are two practical questions which arise in connection with the confession of sin on the part of the believer. First, How may he know what to confess? and second, To whom should he confess?

In answer to the question—How may he know what to confess?—it may be stated that there are at least three ways by which a Christian may come to know his unlikeness to the mind and character of God. These are:

I. The Inscripturated Word

The written Word of God, the teachings of which he may have neglected or transgressed. "All scripture is given by inspiration of God, and is profitable for doctrine, for reproof, for correction, for instruction in righteousness: that the man of God may be perfect, thoroughly furnished unto all good works" (2 Tim. 3:16, 17).

II. Fellow Believers

The faithful admonition of the fellow-members of the body of Christ. "Moreover if thy brother shall trespass against thee, go and tell him his fault between thee and him alone: if he shall hear thee, thou hast gained thy brother. But if he will not hear thee, then take with thee one or two more, that in the mouth of two or three witnesses every word may be established. And if he shall neglect to hear them, tell it unto the church: but if he shall neglect to hear the church, let him be unto thee as an heathen man and a publican" (Matt. 18:15-17). "Take heed to yourselves: if thy brother trespass against thee, rebuke him; and if he repent, forgive him. And if he trespass against thee seven times in a day, and seven times in a day turn again to thee, saying, I repent; Thou shalt forgive him" (Luke 17:3, 4). "Brethren, if a man be overtaken in a fault, ye which are spiritual, restore such an one in the spirit of meekness; considering thyself, lest thou also be tempted" (Gal. 6:1).

III. The Spirit's Prodding

The grieved Spirit Who indwells him. The grieving of the Spirit will be to the Christian as an inner consciousness of wrong, which he must carefully and prayerfully heed. "And grieve not the Holy Spirit of God, whereby ye are sealed unto the day of redemption" (Eph. 4:30).

The child of God will learn to distinguish between the ever-present unlikeness to Christ and the grosser sins that are mentioned in the Bible. "Adultery, fornication, uncleanness, lasciviousness, idolatry, witchcraft, hatred, variance, emulations, wrath, strife, seditions, heresies, envyings, murders, drunkenness, revelings, and such like" (Gal. 5:19-21). In this passage it will be seen that the sins of hatred, wrath, envy, variance, emulations and strife are mentioned in the same list with adultery, murder and drunkenness.

If a Christian really purposes to get right with God at any cost, he may well pray the prayer recorded in Psa. 139:23, 24: "Search me, O God, and know my heart: try me, and know my thoughts: and see if there be any wicked way in me, and lead me in the way everlasting." There is assurance that every unholy thing will be revealed to the one who thus prays. "Let us therefore, as many as be perfect [full grown], be thus minded: and if in anything ye be otherwise minded, God shall reveal even this unto you" (Phil. 3:15).

In answer to this prayer for light upon the hidden sins in the life, there may be but one sin revealed at a time, and further revelations may be made to depend both upon an honest dealing with the revelation already given and upon a repetition of the same supplication. There is no other way for a Christian to deal with his sin-hindered life.

The voice of the unseen enemy must also be detected. He is ever present to dissuade the believer from taking the necessary step that leads him back into fellowship with God, and into the power and blessing of service. Satan's method is to seek to minimize the hindering sin, to justify the unholy act or position, and to appeal to the personal pride of the Christian, or suggest that a confession of sin would hinder the believer's influence for his Lord.

The answer to the second question: "To whom should a Christian confess?" is more simple:

I. To God

Confession of sin should always be to God; for he is wronged by the sin of a Christian more than any mortal. The Scripture examples of confession are clear on this point. "Against thee, Thee only, have I sinned, and done this evil in thy sight" (Psa. 51:4). "I will arise and go to my father, and will say unto him, Father, I have sinned against heaven, and before thee, and am no more worthy to be called thy son: make me as one of thy hired servants" (Luke 15:18,19).

II. To Those Wronged Directly

Confession should be made to the person or persons who have been wronged by the sin. Here, it may be added, confession does not in any way involve the wrong attitude of others, nor does it demand that the responsibility for sin shall be assumed by a person who is in no way at fault. If there has been an enmity between a Christian and some other person, the Christian is asked to consider and confess only his own wrong state of heart or sinful acts. This may not solve the misunderstanding between the two parties, but it will open the way for the cleansing of the Christian who confesses his sins.

Again, confession of sins should always be limited to those who have been wronged, whether the sin has been committed against the community, the church or an individual.

III. To Those Wronged Indirectly

Confession should be made to any who have known of the sin; for they, in a measure, have also been wronged. "And make straight paths for your feet, lest that which is lame be turned out of the way; but let it rather be healed. Follow peace with all men and holiness, without which no man shall see the Lord: looking diligently lest any man fail of the grace of God; lest any root of bitterness springing up trouble you, and thereby many be defiled" (Heb. 12:13-15). "Let us not therefore judge one another any more: but judge this rather, that no man put a stumbling-block or an occasion to fall in his brother's way" (Rom. 14:13; see also Luke 17:1, 2; 1 Cor. 8:7-13).

The fifty-first Psalm is the record of David's repentance and return to fellowship with God after his great sin, and is an exact statement of the necessary steps to be taken by a covenant person in returning to his place of joy and power in service. The Psalm opens with a complete confession of sin; claims the cleansing that is promised; and ends with the restoration to joy, service, and whole fellowship with God.

If there is no fruit borne to the glory of God, no fellowship with God, and no joy in the life of a believer, it is evidence that there is need of adjustment in that life to the mind and will of God. Such adjustments are the common experience of those who know what it is to walk with God; for there is no other way to keep that priceless fellowship and blessing. The secret of abiding in such a walk with God is instant confession of every known sin, rather than a delay in, or an entire neglect of the performance of that duty.

Let it be restated that, while the believer may not be realizing a state of sinless perfection, he can and must maintain an attitude of willing and instant confession of every known wrong, if he would walk in fellowship with his Lord and minister in the priestly office.

When the heart is searched before God, and all sin is put away, the believer will "walk in the light as he is in the light"; for that is the normal, if not the usual, Christian experience. In this relationship there will be fellowship with the Father and with His Son Jesus Christ, a running over with peace and joy, and unhindered outflow of the love of God through the life. [1]

Of this outflow of love it may be stated that, as the love of God is shed abroad in our hearts by the Spirit Which is given unto us, the normal experience of every believer should be a divine sense of the lost condition of unsaved people, which will prompt any necessary sacrifice or effort to win them. The particular person or persons for whom a Christian may be burdened, and the extent of that burden, will be indicated and governed by the sovereign movings of the Spirit of God; while the personal cleansing which conditions the sense of the burden is the one point of responsibility for the believer.

Where the believer-priest is cleansed and is in communion

---

1. A more extended treatment of the believer's life in the Spirit and its necessary conditions will be found in the author's book, *He That Is Spiritual*.

with God, the love of God shed abroad in his heart will create in him a divine longing for the salvation of the lost and this will be brought about by the Spirit "which is given unto him." He will then, from time to time, be driven to intercession and prayer through his suffering with Christ for the lost. Like Paul he will say: "My heart's desire and prayer to God for Israel is, that they might be saved," and this prayer will be an intercession by the Spirit; "For we know not what to pray for as we ought: but the Spirit itself maketh intercession for us with groanings which cannot be uttered." And since that prayer is indicted by the Spirit, Who knows the mind of God, that prayer will be answered by the going forth of the Spirit in power, wielding His mighty sword to convict of sin, of righteousness, and of judgment. Then where this divinely wrought vision is received and acted upon by a depositing of all hope and trust in the Lamb of God that taketh away the sin of the world, there will be, by the same Spirit, a marvelous transformation of the whole estate from the power and darkness of Satan into the light, liberty and blessing of the sons of God.

Thus when the believer-priest is cleansed and in a normal relation to God, the Spirit is free to take every necessary step in the "power of God unto salvation," and the believer will be led into perfect co-operation with Christ in His great unfinished work of seeking the lost. The work is all accomplished by the Spirit; for it is the Spirit Who inspires the prayer which is the only relief for the one who is suffering with Christ through the divinely given burden for the lost; it is the Spirit Who convinces of sin, of righteousness, and of judgment in answer to prayer which He inspires; and it is the Spirit Who meets the willing soul with the power of God in salvation.

True evangelism begins, then, with a cleansed priest, and while this human instrument may cooperate in much of the subsequent work in seeking the lost, he is ever reminded that, "It is not by might, nor by power, but by my Spirit saith the Lord."

Chapter 7
An Appeal

The purpose of this book has been realized if you, its reader, have gained some new vision of a wider field of ministry for your own life, as a Christian, in the God-given, superlative privilege of soul-winning. May the power of the Spirit be so upon you, through your yieldedness to Him, that every new impression or understanding of divine Truth may be actualized in abiding fruit to the glory of our great God and Savior Jesus Christ.

Index of Scripture Texts

Subject Index